# Pro
# Perspectives

## Examining Beliefs, Biases, and Reality Through Stories

By

**Steve Gill**

**Ushani Nanayakkara**

Thank You for Your Support!

Steve

Cover photo by Ushani Nanayakkara
What is this photo? See last page for the answer.

# Acknowledgments

We would like to thank the people who provided stories, both those who were willing to be identified and those who wanted to be anonymous. Some of these stories are very personal to the individuals who wrote them. Even as successful adults, many are not interested in talking about their own struggles in life or the struggles of their children. In some cases, the struggles are or were painful. Yet, they wanted to share their stories in the hope of helping others, especially children.

The following people either provided valuable feedback during the process of writing this book, provided a story, or both (noting some people are anonymous by their choice). A special thanks to the following people: Rebekah Hereth, Toni Palsson, Carolyn Workman, Mustafa Abdirahman, Heather Matthews, Adrienne Adzanku, Amrinder Bains, Tracy Pennington, Laurie Harrison, Steve Hirsch, and Gretchen Henry.

# Table of Contents

# Preface

In education and psychology, the popular saying "their perception is their reality" surfaced several years ago. This was, and to some extent still is, a very valuable tool in helping to understand interactions and behaviors of others. Sadly, it has lost some of its value due to forgetting that perception is not actually reality, in many cases.

When there is a robbery at a store and the police interview people, they run into the problem of perception versus reality. They will have almost as many versions of what occurred as there are witnesses. The witnesses will vary on virtually every detail, from what occurred, to what the person was wearing, to how tall they might have been (this is why there are height charts on the door jams of some businesses).

This is a problem when two individuals or two groups of individuals are trying to solve a problem. It is hard to solve a problem when you don't actually know what the root cause is, given you are not even sure what actually happened.

In education, we have significant issues with disproportionality, be it discipline rates, qualification rates for special education, qualification rates for gifted education, access to programs, etc. The authors believe a great deal of this is due to belief systems.

We all have belief systems that have developed based upon how we were acculturated and the knowledge we gained as we grew up. These belief systems were solidified and modified as we were educated, and as we worked. In almost all cases, people are not doing anything purposefully to hurt others, or to limit others' access to valuable programs, yet it is occurring. Therefore, we need to examine our belief systems.

The following stories, reflections and appendices provide other ways, other perceptions, in which to look at many issues.

The stories were written by individuals who have had success within the areas they are addressing.

We want to allow our data to determine our success and then try to emulate what leads to better results for everyone involved. To do this, we have to examine whether or not what we believe to be "real" is only our perception. We, at times, must change our beliefs to change our behaviors.

# Introduction

The following stories and reflections represent some of the lessons learned and experiences encountered along the course of a career, actually several careers. The hope is that each one of these stories can either inspire the reader to look at a certain situation differently or that the reader can use the story to help others see a certain situation differently.

These stories or reflections on topics were either written by the authors or submitted to the authors. These thoughts on important topics were sometimes emails to staff to encourage or provoke thinking on a difficult topic. In some cases, the person submitting the story had little or no desire to be known as the author of the story, or even demanded anonymity. In some cases, there is more story and in some cases there is more reflection.

The authors love the usage of stories, given that stories are such a traditional means to share knowledge. Also, stories tend to bring out emotions, and emotions help us to solidify memories.

For example, parents often try to teach their 3-4-year-old children some word that they think is very, very important. However, the child does not see things quite the same way, and they don't learn this "important" new word. Then, while the parent is driving down the road, someone cuts them off, and the parent responds with "!*& @%*&**^." The following day, probably in front of the grandparents or best friends, the little darling will repeat that same phrase, with the correct usage, intonation, and emotion. They only heard the phrase once.

Emotions have a powerful effect on learning and memory.

Another strength to stories is that they allow the reader to be both a smart and smarter person at the same time. Growing up, one of the authors heard the following line repeatedly: "a smart person learns from their mistakes, a smarter person learns from their mistakes *and* the mistakes of others." We have no idea what the source is for that quote, and it could have been Steve's grandfather who made it up. Either way, stories allow the reader to learn from the adventures of others.

The thoughts on topics coved within these stories are provided by people who have shown success and are leaders in the area they are talking about.

## The hope for this book

The authors hope that school psychologists, teachers, principals and others use these stories both on a personal and professional level. Each of these stories will start with an introduction regarding "what to look for" and end with suggested reflections. These stories have been chosen for their potential to help individuals and groups see that the line, "your perspective is your reality" or "the student's perspective is their reality" can be looked at differently. Sometimes our reality, our perspectives are based upon either a lack of experience or a lack of knowledge and we need to grow and learn. This book will hopefully provide a safe environment for people to explore by reading and processing some very personal stories, and some not as personal, and see that this lens of perspective at times needs some cleaning.

## How to use this book

The stories in this book can be used solely for personal growth, but can also be used to help colleagues and for teaching purposes. The following paragraphs provide examples of using a specific story for helping colleagues or for teaching purposes.

If you are a teacher, school psychologist or a principal who leads training, you can use many of these stories as discussion starters. For example, the story/discussion on communication can be used in a training or staff meetings in order to start discussions within groups. After people have read the story(s), they can discuss with their table partners the questions noted in the book. Then, after they have done that, they can summarize what they have learned as a group. This can be followed by sharing out to the larger group. In the end, the group can talk about norms they want to use in order to ensure higher levels of effective communication.

If you are a teacher, school psychologist or a principal in a building in which you have great people doing great things for difficult kids, and it is near the end of the year, and you see people wearing out, you can leverage the story about compassion fatigue. This is a concept that most people have experience with, but few people ever talk about or address. This happens when people are dealing with someone who is rather difficult and/or draining over a long period of time, and they have been doing a great job, but they are just running out of compassion. As they run out of compassion, they will tend to react to things differently than they had before. This can be profoundly confusing to the person who is difficult and/or draining, given that they might repeat the same behaviors as before and get totally different results.

Some issues that we deal with drain our energy very, very slowly. As this occurs, we are usually unaware of the impact on us and we are usually unaware of how our own behaviors change. Therefore, the simple act of naming what has occurred and seeing that other people have gone through similar struggles can provide us with new insights, and often the ability to dig deeper into our reserves for the energy needed to help the individual who is draining our energy. Also, seeing the concept written about in a book will help to validate the feelings, and that validation encourages us to dig deeper into our reserves, or know when to "tap-in" another person. As care givers, we need to never forget to take care of ourselves. Therefore, there might be times in which we need to ask another person to help for a while, while we regain the needed strength to continue our work.

## Themes

As you use this book and read the different stories, please try to think about themes that span the different stories. What are the things that people keep doing that lead to different and better results? What are the things that people tend to do that lead to poor results, struggles to grow, or poor behaviors?

# First story:

# What is a disability???

The following story was written by someone who was told by doctors and others that they have a disability. However, that person happens to see things a little differently. It is possible that their view of what constitutes a disability would help many children….

**Things to think about when reading this story:**

- As you read this story, can you relate to it personally?
- Have you ever worked with a student, colleague or parent who was similar?
- What messages did you send to that student, colleague, or parent verbally or non-verbally?
- How do you believe they remember you?
- How would you like to be remembered by them?
- What did you do to make their life better?
- What did you do that might not have made their life better?

## What is a disability???

It was just over 20 years ago when I woke up on a Saturday morning and my left arm no longer worked. I could get it to wiggle, but nothing more than that. Also, my left hand wasn't able to do much and I was struggling to feel anything with my right hand.

About 2 years before this, I had been sent to a series of doctors, all trying to figure out what was going on with some weird problems I was having. I was really struggling with some fine motor issues and having some extreme headaches. Most of the doctors blamed this on the hard style, old school Karate training that I had been doing for years. However, one of the doctors didn't just write it off as easily. This doctor sent me to a neurologist who sent me in for a test that my neurosurgeon later said would have been used as a torture technique if some folks had known about it. They eventually figured out that I had fractured my neck, probably in a car accident that I had been in, and I had bone spurs growing inside my spinal canal. These bone spurs were cutting off nerve function to my left arm and hand, and my right hand.

At the time, I was about 30 years old and the doctor told me, "the insurance company will not authorize the surgery given your age and you do not have a major life impact." So, they sent me home. Then, about 2 years later, I woke up that morning with a major life impact. Given I was only 32 at the time, they decided to put me through about 6 months of different drug trials and other stuff that was of ZERO use. Then, I had the surgery.

Due to those interesting twists and turns, I was left with lifelong problems. I have never regained full usage of my left arm, left hand, or right hand.

However, things aren't too bad.

In the year following the surgery, the headaches had virtually disappeared. Those were easily the most brutal headaches I could have ever imagined, and they stopped me from functioning on many days. As time progressed, I was having an easier and easier time with some fine motor activities. For example, it took me about a year to be able to button a dress shirt without watching myself, my hands, in the mirror. I had one shirt that buttoned on the other side than normal for a men's shirt, I threw it away!!! It took me about a year to be able to put a coin in a pop machine without using two hands. If I didn't use two hands I would frequently let go of the coin before it actually was in the slot far enough to fall into the machine.

Do I have a disability? I was asked, a couple of years ago: what do you think is a disability? I had thought about this for a long period of time prior to ever being asked the question. To me, a disability is something that stops you from doing what you want to do.

So, what is it that I cannot do anymore? Nothing that I know of. However, there are things that are so frustrating that I just stopped trying. I used to do a lot of work on old cars, but I couldn't continue that. I stopped playing golf, mostly because of my ego, though. I only have about a half of a swing, which means I lost about 70-80 yards off of the tee, and that was driving me crazy. But, I am starting up again. I have good and bad days with my handwriting. Some days I literally have to watch my hand as I write the letters, willing my hand to make the correct shapes. Sometimes people make fun of me for my struggles with hand writing, until they understand the reason.

I am lucky. My problems and challenges are small when compared to many people. Most people who break their necks have much bigger challenges than I have.

The Para Olympics are a good example of many, many people who are considered to have disabilities doing things that others would find impossible to believe that a person with a "disability" could possibly do.

So, I am not sure "what a disability is" for the next person, but to me a disability is something that stops a person from doing what they want to do. Sadly, though, for many people the disability is put upon them by others telling them what they cannot or should not do, in place of saying, "let's figure it out." I am sure glad my age has overcome my ego, so I can try golfing again. It is a rare occasion that you get to hit something as hard as you can and find joy in watching it fly off.

What would happen if we spent our time trying to help children and adults with disabilities try to figure out what they can do, how they can modify an activity, in order to find purpose and joy?

**Reflection:**

Now that you have read the story and thought about the questions, it is time to reflect.

- What did you think about when you read this story?
- How can that help you in dealing with current and future students?
- How can that help you in dealing with current and future parents?
- How can that help you in dealing with current and future colleagues?
- What can you do differently starting today, to achieve better results (even if you started with good results)?

# Living with a Disability

There are times in which we become frustrated when trying to teach or deal with students, or adults, who have disabilities. However, no matter the struggles that we face in these situations, we do not face the kinds of challenges these individuals face when living with their disabilities.

**Things to think about when reading this story:**

- As you read this story, can you relate to it personally?
- Have you ever worked with a student, colleague or parent who was similar?
- What messages did you send to that student, colleague, or parent verbally or non-verbally?
- How do you believe they remember you?
- How would you like to be remembered by them?
- What did you do to make their life better?
- What did you do that might not have made their life better?

### Living with a Disability

Imagine being a little kid and everyone making fun of you, people telling you that you are stupid, then believing that what everyone called a disability had just kind of disappeared as you grew up. What if a change in your life brought all of those same problems back to life, and you learned that the "disability" wasn't gone, you just had strategies to deal with it under most circumstances? What if you happen to be lucky enough to have grown up to learn about and work with children with disabilities, and can see this whole problem from a totally different perspective?

This is my life, my adventure, and it sure has not been a simple one.

As a child, I could not effectively communicate with anyone. This was very frustrating, I can remember that part of it. I can also remember being told I was dumb, retarded. What I don't remember was the day in which my family found out I was not "dumb." I was told I was dumb, retarded, and the story of how my parents found out otherwise is one my grandmother told me many times over the years.

My parents had been convinced by their friends that "he must be retarded, he makes no sense…." After hearing this over time, they eventually scheduled an evaluation with Children's Hospital in Seattle. The first person to see me was a Speech and Language Pathologist. This person told my parents that not only was I not "retarded," I might be reasonably bright. That afternoon I was evaluated by either Nancy or Hal Robinson (they later went on to found the Robinson Center on the University of Washington Campus, and many years later I taught in that program). They told my parents that I was rather bright. However, that did not change my ability to communicate. I still had extreme articulation issues and additionally they told my parents I have Aphasia (SLPs have argued that it is unlikely that I have Aphasia, but one SLP did some research and found a version of Aphasia that matches my symptoms).

Life progressed and I received enormous quantities of speech and language therapy. I learned a lot of ways to deal with the problems that I faced, and I pretty much forgot about having a "disability."

Throughout my adult life I have struggled with confidence, but I somehow was gifted a level of "stubbornness" that is able to overcome the self-doubts. It is pretty hard to grow up hearing that you are stupid, dumb, retarded and not have some residual affects, or is that effects? Depends, I guess, on perspective. I started getting A's in school in the 9th grade (once the grades mattered). And, I had an A average from high school, through undergraduate work, and through graduate work. Yet, I still showed up early for every test, so that I could go through self-talk. It went something like this, "you have done this before, this is not any different, you are prepared, you can do this....."

Yet, I was not relating this to my "disability," until I started trying to learn Spanish in my early 40's. I was lucky, a leading expert told me a way to learn the language (Stephen Krashen and comprehensible input, if you want to look it up). My Spanish took off pretty darn good. After a few years, my understanding and my ability to read was going great, but I was terrified to talk. My stubborn side had me trying, but it was quite the struggle. Over the years, I have gone to school in Spain and Mexico, and I have achieved a very high level in my Spanish studies, but I still had this underlying problem, this underlying doubt. I was still struggling with my ability to pronounce words in Spanish.

It was not until this last summer, in Spain, that I learned what was going on. In a nutshell, my struggles to say some words correctly (not knowledge, but my articulation disability) were making people believe that my skills were lower than they really are. This past summer, I told my Spanish teachers about my disability. This allowed them to see my skills and separate those from my disability. So, here I am in my 50's and I am still having people see me as less capable due to my disability.

While all of this was occurring, I have become an expert in the area of ELL and Special Education. A system that I created and wrote my first book on has become widely used across Washington State and is being used in many other states as well. As of spring 2018 I have trained roughly 8,000 educators on ELL/Special Education issues. In other words, I have done a *ton* of public speaking, sometimes with over 300 people in the crowd. I often have to speak for up to 6 ½ hours in one day on these topics. Almost nobody ever notices my disability, except the Speech and Language Pathologists. However, I notice every mistake I make. The errors with articulation are things that everyone can hear and notice, but our normal filters have us ignoring a lot of those problems.

One of my problems, though, is that my articulation can have bad days, especially when I am tired.

With the aphasia, or whatever it is, I have a lot of strategies in English. What most people have noted is that it appears that I have paused to either make an emphasis or to pick just the right wording. The truth is that I am running through my bank of synonyms to try to find a word to replace that other word with, the word that I know but cannot say. This is the worst with nouns, the worst with people's names. There are times in which I just cannot find the word or a synonym. There are times in which I can literally see the word in front of me, but it will not come out. Yet, in English, I make my way through these challenges and everything works out. In Spanish, though, my bank of synonyms is not as large. Therefore, people think that I just don't know the word (lack of skill or knowledge, in place of a disability).

Now, where is all of this going? I have recently seen a couple of TEDx talks, one from a woman with CP and one from a woman with ADHD. Also, I have been asked many times, given I talk to groups about disabilities, what I think a disability is. In my case and the case of these two women, we all have something we have to overcome to achieve what we want to achieve. We all have people who treat us poorly at times based upon something we have very little control over. We have all found our way to some level of success, all while our "disabilities" try to slow us down.

To me, a disability is something that you cannot work around, something that stops you from doing a specific activity. For many people, paralysis stops them from physical activities they would like to do. However, for others, they find a way to get as close as possible to the activities through work-arounds. So, I would like to close this with asking everyone to look at people with "disabilities" differently. What if, instead of calling someone dumb (or thinking it) or telling someone that cannot do something (or thinking it), we all tried to help the person look for ways in which they could achieve their goals.

As a fairly successful adult, I can tell you that very well educated and well-meaning people have treated me as "less able" throughout my life. Some people will read parts of this story and think "never me." So, before saying "not me," check your thoughts and actions the next time someone is struggling with a skill in front of you.

I wrote this mostly for myself. That is, I wrote it as part of trying to understand my journey and to be something cathartic. I am struggling to find or think of a way to share my experience, so that children and adults can in some way benefit from knowing how others have felt, how others have survived, how others have thrived. Yet, I am struggling to put my own name on this, given I still do not really want to talk much about this journey, except with people close to me or when I believe that the sharing can help someone else. If you do happen to read this, maybe you can help. Either with your interactions with people who are struggling or with ways to share the message. Thank you for your time.

**Reflection:**

Now that you have read the story and thought about the questions, it is time to reflect.

- What did you think about when you read this story?
- How can that help you in dealing with current and future students?
- How can that help you in dealing with current and future parents?
- How can that help you in dealing with current and future colleagues?
- What can you do differently starting today, to achieve better results (even if you started with good results)?

# Even Our Most Difficult Kids...

The following is a story about how a very difficult child thrived in a school that worked very hard to build a relationship with the child.

### Things to think about when reading this story:

- As you read this story, can you relate to it personally?
- Have you ever worked with a student, colleague or parent who was similar?
- What messages did you send to that student, colleague, or parent verbally or non-verbally?
- How do you believe they remember you?
- How would you like to be remembered by them?
- What did you do to make their life better?
- What did you do that might not have made their life better?

## Even Our Most Difficult Kids…

The toughest of kids might need a relationship more than anyone else.

I was simply amazed that this truly petite, beautiful little girl could be so difficult.

First, a little bit about her and her journey through life to help you understand what was going on. This little girl is one of the many children that her mother had with numerous different fathers. Due to her mother's struggles with alcohol and drugs, this child spent much of her early life in and out of shelters, and of course in situations where drugs and/or alcohol were being abused. In the school system, she was labeled as behaviorally disabled before she even entered kindergarten. Her IEP didn't even describe any services for her, it just said "self-contained special education for 1,500 minutes per week." She came to our school as a ____-year-old. When our school psychologist called the previous school district, they really couldn't tell him anything that they had done with this little girl. We, as a school, decided to keep her in a general education setting. We quickly found out that she had virtually no exposure to reading, math or writing, prior to arriving. Therefore, she had no skills in these areas. We made a very unusual decision (with the support of her foster care family), and we moved her back a grade.

First, this little girl, cute as can be and wearing the prettiest of clothes, just flat out refused to do what we told her multiple times per day. Instead, she just stood in place and acted like we didn't exist. Therefore, it really was not the most disruptive of behaviors.

As time progressed, she began to develop relationships with different individuals within our school. Therefore, the refusal behaviors started to decrease in intensity and other interesting behaviors came to life. For example, this little darling had the stickiest of fingers. She stole one of just about everything. Luckily for us, she really wasn't very good at it and she even got herself into trouble on more than one occasion by bragging about what she "had."

A big part of finding success with her was making sure to let her shine. We figured out what she was good at and made sure she had the opportunity to do this in front of others. In my class, we have a math routine that we do each day. At first, I was a little worried about having her leading this, given her struggles with reading and math. However, I soon learned that she had been paying special attention to our routine. It was amazing to watch her run this activity, she asked all the right questions and did a great job calling on students during the activity.

Working with her on her reluctance to complete work was another trick to be had. I really needed to figure out what she liked and then do the old "first _____, then _____." She liked to read the geography examples. So, I would let her read the first one. Then, she wanted to read more. I told her that she had to write the answers to the next 3 items before she could have another turn.

It is very important to note that none of this would have occurred if it were not for the relationship we were building over time. I know that she understood how much we (I) cared about her, given she always wanted a hug each and every day. Remember, this is one tough little girl we are talking about. Also, my school psychologist recently told me about listening to us talk when she was in trouble. He told me, and I believe this, that children are incredibly good at hearing the message our voice is giving, well beyond the words that we say. In other words, your voice will give away whether or not you really like a child, no matter the words that you choose. He said that, even when it was clear that I was very unhappy with what she had done (based upon my words), that he could still hear the care and love in my voice. It goes back to that old saying, "I don't like what you did, but I still like you."

This little girl, over the course of a couple of years, has made tremendous growth. Was she extremely difficult at times? YES! Can she still be rather naughty at times? YES! But, she is a great example of how caring relationships have not only allowed her to avoid having to be in a classroom for students with behavioral disabilities, but also how caring relationships have helped her to grow and learn in ways many people thought were impossible.

It is also important to note that she has made strong academic growth during this time, too. She, like so many kids and adults, works harder and harder as she is finding success, "success breeds success." She still doesn't like to read; however, she is much more willing to read if she is reading one-to-one with an adult who she likes. Like so many children with behavioral issues, she seeks attention. Reading with an adult she likes is very positive attention. Like so many kids with behavioral issues, she is willing to have either positive or negative attention. Therefore, it is so critical to create opportunities for positive attention. And, the more often we can do this, the less time she has to seek or participate in anything that includes negative attention.

On a side note, her foster family thinks we walk on water. Therefore, we don't have to have those "fights" that sometimes occur with families when a little one does something inappropriate. Instead, they understand that we care, and they trust us.

**Reflection:**

Now that you have read the story and thought about the questions, it is time to reflect.

- What did you think about when you read this story?
- How can that help you in dealing with current and future students?
- How can that help you in dealing with current and future parents?
- How can that help you in dealing with current and future colleagues?
- What can you do differently starting today, to achieve better results (even if you started with good results)?

# A Phone Call and Some Background Knowledge...

Sometimes our fears and reluctance to make phone calls to address difficult situations can limit our knowledge, and that can greatly limit our success. Also, knowing a person's history can completely change our impression of their behaviors.

**Things to think about when reading this story:**

- As you read this story, can you relate to it personally?
- Have you ever worked with a student, colleague or parent who was similar?
- What messages did you send to that student, colleague, or parent verbally or non-verbally?
- How do you believe they remember you?
- How would you like to be remembered by them?
- What did you do to make their life better?
- What did you do that might not have made their life better?

## A phone call and some background knowledge…

I was working away in my office one day when a teacher stopped by to tell me about how horrible this one girl was behaving and how difficult she is in class. We talked for a while, and the behavior really was pretty bad behavior. In a nutshell, she presented as extremely negative and pretty darn nasty. So, I asked the teacher what she knew about this girl, and the reality was that she knew almost nothing about her. I asked her about calling home, and there was no way she was going to do this.

During my career as a _____, I have had several teachers and some school psychologists show great resistance to calling the family of a child who is presenting like this young lady. There are all kinds of horror stories about the families attacking the teacher or school psychologist who dares to call the house and say that the child is not behaving like a perfect little angel. In many of these cases, these families are just tired of hearing negatives.

I volunteered to call the family, and this was a moment in my career that I will never forget.

When I called the home, I asked to speak to "Suzy's" mother or father (Suzy was not her real name). The person I reached said that that was impossible. When I asked her why, she said that the father had beaten the mother to death, and he was in prison for it. It took me a moment or three to gather my composure and continue with the conversation. As we continued, I learned that "Suzy" had actually been in the room and witnessed this occur. And, since that time she had had very little counseling and no work to deal with the trauma. This was pretty early in my career, so I ended up calling everyone I could think of for advice.

As a team, we met and talked about how we were going to work with Suzy moving forward. We found out that none of her friends and nobody in the school setting knew this information about her. We didn't share anything with other students, obviously, but within a small group of teachers, administrators, counselors and the school psychologist we shared the information. This was long before all of the current work on dealing with trauma in children became so popular, and it is very possible we made mistakes along the way. We encouraged her grandmother to seek counseling and trauma treatment, and provided her the names of resources to contact.

A few of us talked directly with the child to tell her that we knew what had occurred and let her know that we were here to attempt to help. Her first question was about whether or not her teachers knew, because they had all started treating her totally differently (with kid gloves). She did not like this and felt that she was being treated with pity. We worked on this with her and her teachers. It was very clear that she was not ready and did not want to talk about her experience, yet.

However, in our efforts, it was clear that she saw adults doing the best they could to provide a caring and supportive environment for her. Her behavior improved remarkably over a short period of time. She was still an unhappy child, but an unhappy child with a glimpse of hope and positivity.

This all came out of a phone call and an effort to understand. We likely made mistakes, but we clearly acted as caring adults trying to make her life a little bit better.

In our careers, we will find times in which a little bit of knowledge completely changes our view of a situation. And, as our view of a situation changes, it is highly likely our behaviors will change as well. This provides an opportunity for a spiral in a positive direction that can lead to much better results.

**Reflection:**

Now that you have read the story and thought about the questions, it is time to reflect.

- What did you think about when you read this story?
- How can that help you in dealing with current and future students?
- How can that help you in dealing with current and future parents?
- How can that help you in dealing with current and future colleagues?
- What can you do differently starting today, to achieve better results (even if you started with good results)?

# Believing In Each Other

The following is a story of a young teacher who went to New Orleans during their recovery from Hurricane Katrina. It illustrates how her belief in her students and their belief in her led to amazing results.

**Things to think about when reading this story:**

- As you read this story, can you relate to it personally?
- Have you ever worked with a student, colleague or parent who was similar?
- What messages did you send to that student, colleague, or parent verbally or non-verbally?
- How do you believe they remember you?
- How would you like to be remembered by them?
- What did you do to make their life better?
- What did you do that might not have made their life better?

### Believing In Each Other

John Hattie is often considered the top researcher in education with regards to what works and does not work in improving student achievement. His research, which is based upon studying the research of others and putting it all together, shows that students who believe in their teachers and teachers who believe in their students are two of the most powerful components to success.

So, there I was, a young white-skinned woman teaching in New Orleans soon after Hurricane Katrina had devastated the area. I was teaching in a classroom in which almost all of my students were black. The only reason I mention this is that part of my story is about building trust, and some of these students didn't have a history of white people seeing them as smart and capable.

At the time in Louisiana, if a student didn't pass a 4th grade skills test, they repeated the 4th grade and they only moved on if they had already failed the test twice. So, in my 6th grade classroom I had students from the age of 11 to the age of 16.

When we started the year in August, we started with very low core academic skills. Many of these students lost a great deal of their core and critical education during the recovery from Hurricane Katrina. For example, in the area of math, some of my students didn't know what the equal sign meant, and for most students I was starting with single-digit addition. But, I saw this as where we were, and not a sign of the skills of my children, my students. Then, a great thing occurred for my students early in the school year. Our hard work led to them having the highest math scores on one of the first tests. In our area, many schools had students who were struggling with the after effects of Hurricane Katrina. However, this let my students see that they were capable learners, smart kids.

As I noted, we started our math with first grade math skills, single-digit addition. In April, we had to take the 6th grade skills test, and 90% of my students passed this test at the 6th grade mastery level. The remaining 10% of my students passed at the 5th grade mastery level. We were extremely excited and proud of these results.

Someone recently asked me, "What do you attribute the success to?" The first thing I said was confidence. My students needed to see themselves as capable learners and they needed to see me as a capable teacher. Doing well on that first test really got us rolling in the right direction! This has nothing to do with a poster hanging in the room or telling kids phrases that you have learned from some textbook. This came from them working very hard and from me working very hard to help them. This also came from building trust.

At that time in New Orleans, we were expected to give out our personal cell phone number. The students would call me on a regular basis, and we would work out math problems together. It is important to note, they were great about having this opportunity, no late phone calls and no prank calls. However, try to imagine what it is like to attempt to teach or tutor long division over the phone.

Another aspect of this was that they could see that I cared about them. Their ability to reach me and get some extra help from me at any reasonable time was critical to this. Also, they knew that I had left my family and friends, and moved there because I wanted to help them. Someone once said, "They don't care how much you know until they know how much you care." It is important for me to express that I didn't go there with some idealistic belief that I was saving these "poor" kids as a "hero." I went there to help and learn. At the time, New Orleans was not only physically rebuilding their schools, but also taking this time to rebuild their educational system. Therefore, it was an amazing learning opportunity for me, working with some amazing educators. Last, these kids provided me with a wonderful experience and helped me to learn a great deal about their culture and about the culture of New Orleans.

This was an amazing experience that I will carry with me throughout my teaching career. It helped me to see how crucial it is to help our children see themselves as capable learners. Furthermore, it reinforced to me how crucial it is to build trusting relationships (especially given what they had gone through), and this helped me to see how vital it is that students know that we care.

I believe it is critical for kids in tough situations to know that there are no excuses. There is a big difference between a "reason" and an "excuse." The reason that their skills were low is that they didn't have the exposure to what they needed to learn, and possibly because they didn't believe in themselves as capable learners. An excuse only slows down getting to work, and that work is what is needed to bridge the gap between doesn't yet know something and passing a test many of these kids would have never believed they could pass.

We must believe in our kids as capable learners, and teach them to believe in themselves as capable learners. It works out better for everyone involved.

**Reflection:**

Now that you have read the story and thought about the questions, it is time to reflect.

- What did you think about when you read this story?
- How can that help you in dealing with current and future students?
- How can that help you in dealing with current and future parents?
- How can that help you in dealing with current and future colleagues?
- What can you do differently starting today, to achieve better results (even if you started with good results)?

## Assume Positive Intent

In our work and within our lives we will deal with a lot of people who present as angry and frustrated, we interact with people whose behaviors do not present as well meaning. However, if we assume positive intent we will have better long-term results than if we allow the presenting behaviors to stop us from looking deeper and attempting to understand the underlying and root causes, of behaviors.

### Things to think about when reading this story:

- As you read this story, can you relate to it personally?
- Have you ever worked with a student, colleague or parent who was similar?
- What messages did you send to that student, colleague, or parent verbally or non-verbally?
- How do you believe they remember you?
- How would you like to be remembered by them?
- What did you do to make their life better?
- What did you do that might not have made their life better?

## Assume Positive Intent

As school psychologists, we have a difficult job, a job that we can make easier or harder depending upon our own beliefs and how we approach life.

We are going to be faced with a large number of people who approach us with negativity of one type or another, and we have to somehow navigate through this. How we choose to react and the belief systems we bring with us, can impact us in a positive or negative manner. If we are not careful real negativity can cause us to see or believe there is negativity where it does not exist. That is, we can start to believe there is bad intent in the majority of the actions around us, because of our approach, when it really is rather rare.

An important point, before going into the heart of the matter, is whether or not the negativity that we believe exists is really negativity at all. I have been lucky enough, or unlucky enough, to have been assigned to take over evaluations from teams in schools. One of these situations was placed onto my plate via a hearing settlement agreement. The school instantly contacted me to tell me how the father was difficult, impossible, angry, etc.... I called the father to talk with him, and told him that I would be calling him 4-5 times before discussing the evaluation at all. He, in what appeared to be a rather angry voice, asked me "why?" I explained to him that I wanted to understand his perspective on the situation and I didn't think he would be ready to tell me until after we had visited for a while. He eventually provided me very valuable information. Was he angry? Yes, he was! However, he had a lot of valid points and information. So, what appears to be negativity could actually be frustration that has a very valid basis.

Another example is that some of the teachers we work with may appear angry and aggressive, but behind this may just be fear and frustration. They are under tremendous pressure to achieve certain results, and they have a student (the student who they might refer for a special education evaluations) who is not achieving, and this worries them. They are hoping and believing special education can help the child in ways that they are not currently able to help the child.

The point is, surface emotions can have root causes that we need to understand, and we cannot allow the surface emotions to stop us from getting to the needed information. If we do not assume positive intent, it is extremely unlikely that we will even look for the information we need.

Assuming positive intent is far different than either assuming negative intent or even just not assuming positive intent. A popular area of discussion these days is microaggressions. With microaggressions there may be an assumption of negative intent. What sometimes follows is the offended person finds the first person they can to tell about the microaggression. What if, in place of this, the person assumed positive intent. It is highly likely that many of the things that are called microaggressions are in fact a lack of knowledge or awareness on the behalf of the speaker. What if, instead of the person who is offended running off to tell one of their friends, they actually approached the speaker and said, "Help me understand what you meant when you said _____." If you are the person who has said something that bothered the other person, be a good listener. Personally, I hate making mistakes and sometimes my initial response to making a mistake is poor. Then, I remember, making mistakes is just part of life. The person who is sharing in order to help build understanding has a tough job, maybe something they have to do often. Therefore, if we are the person who has offended, we need to strive to make things easier for them, hoping that they will feel more comfortable sharing, which increases the likelihood of mutual understanding.

Microaggressions do really occur at times, and they are mentally and emotionally taxing experiences for those who are the target of these errors. We must be careful that the burden of educating people does not always fall upon those on the receiving end of microaggressions. Everyone needs to strive to be aware of their own biases and to educate themselves, especially when someone is offended. We can ask ourselves, "Did I miss something about this person's background, culture, personal experiences, or lifestyle that is contributing to these miscommunications? What do I need to understand about this person so that we can address the deeper issues, rather than just the surface emotions?" This may involve asking the person questions, or doing research of your own. Sometimes a little personal research can go a long way in showing your positive intent.

As school psychologists, one of the skills we are supposed to grow is collaboration. A big part of collaboration is seeking to understand, before seeking to be understood. Therefore, we need to approach situations with the belief that people have positive intent. Approaching all situations with this belief is likely to lead to high levels of success. Instances in which someone truly did not demonstrate positive intent should be few and far in-between. In contrast, approaching our work with the lens of "not assuming positive intent" can and will blind us to the many possibilities for the behaviors we are seeing.

Another area in which an open mind and open heart is critical is working with children who are difficult to work with, and, in all honesty, sometimes difficult to like. If we cannot see beyond those surface behaviors, if we cannot control our emotions that arise from what these children say, we cannot find success with these children. These children need us as much or more than any other children, yet they will stretch our abilities and beliefs to new levels. Some of these children will approach us with very unpleasant commentary, far beyond "microaggressions" and even beyond "macroaggressions." They will find our weaknesses and attack them. However, what if it is all a test to see whether or not we will stick it out with them? For some of these children, they don't want to take a chance on a relationship with you, if they believe you will run away once things get deep. So, if we cannot learn to address microaggressions, and even macroaggressions, with people who are not truly intending an aggression, how can we possibly learn to help these children who are being aggressive, but are doing so as an act of as self-preservation.

We have a difficult job!

Let's not make it more difficult by seeing negativity and bad intent all around us.

Let's make it easier by assuming positive intent and having the courage to approach others and have what can be difficult discussions. I would much rather solve most problems and grow with most people, because I assumed positive intent, knowing that on rare occasions I will be wrong about the intent of the person I am working with.

As educators, all of us are good people trying to do good things. The vast, vast majority of our parents are good people, doing the best that they can.

**Reflection:**

Now that you have read the story and thought about the questions, it is time to reflect.

- What did you think about when you read this story?
- How can that help you in dealing with current and future students?
- How can that help you in dealing with current and future parents?
- How can that help you in dealing with current and future colleagues?
- What can you do differently starting today, to achieve better results (even if you started with good results)?

# Compassion Fatigue

As helping professionals, we are often faced with helping individuals who are difficult to help. They may be difficult to help because their disability makes progress so difficult for them or they may be difficult to help because their behaviors are so draining on the helpers. During this, it is natural to struggle to maintain continued compassion. We need to acknowledge this and learn to effectively deal with it.

## Things to think about when reading this story:

- As you read this story, can you relate to it personally?
- Have you ever worked with a student, colleague or parent who was similar?
- What messages did you send to that student, colleague, or parent verbally or non-verbally?
- How do you believe they remember you?
- How would you like to be remembered by them?
- What did you do to make their life better?
- What did you do that might not have made their life better?

## Compassion Fatigue

The end of the school year always brings challenges, yet this year we might be facing additional challenges in the area of compassion fatigue. It is very normal for us to get worn out when it comes to working with students who have many challenges that make our jobs as educators even more "interesting."

This year, though, we have one family who has gone through many problems and tough times. So, instead of our normal number of students for whom we may be experiencing compassion fatigue, we have an abnormally high number of students. That is, there are many children in this family and they are all struggling.

These students struggled on many levels. Then, the death of one parent and another parent being placed into prison transformed these sweet kids with limited skills to not so sweet kids with limited skills. It is hard enough to be a student who struggles greatly to read, write and to do math. However, if those same students lost a parent to violence and another went to prison, their struggles would naturally multiply.

The school staff was able to show a great deal of compassion throughout about ¾ of the school year. Then, the truly unpleasant behavior of these students began to weigh on the staff. It is hard for a teacher to continue to show compassion, after hearing for the Nth time that they are a, "dumb ass bitch." Nevertheless, we worked hard with these children to help them know we cared about them, we just didn't like some of their behaviors. We accomplished this through small and consistent actions, like letting them know, first thing in the morning, that today is a new day and tomorrow is behind us (if the day before had been a hard day).

Many years earlier I worked with the best teacher I have ever met with regards to having difficult children in his classroom. The funny part, though, was his compassion lasted until ten days

46

before the end of the school year, every year. That's when his compassion was totally fatigued.

These students present with many different behaviors that take a great deal of energy from us while we ensure that we are doing everything we can to provide them access to their education. A key factor is that they, at their age, really do not fully understand that their behaviors are in part created due to events beyond their control. However, as the educators we understand that these challenging behaviors are a natural response to what these children face in their lives. This does not make it easier for us in regards to the amount of work we must put in. However, the additional understanding that we have helps us dig to deeper and deeper levels as we combat the stresses we face as a year comes to an end. Know that your feelings and stress are real and reasonable byproducts of the tough work we do. Also, know that our students are counting on us to somehow find that extra level of energy and understanding. Take care of yourself, visit with an understanding friend, get out into nature, whatever it is that you find regenerates your energy. And, know that we have done this before and we can do it again!!!!

**Reflection:**

- Now that you have read the story and thought about the questions, it is time to reflect.
- What did you think about when you read this story?
- How can that help you in dealing with current and future students?
- How can that help you in dealing with current and future parents?
- How can that help you in dealing with current and future colleagues?
- What can you do differently starting today, to achieve better results (even if you started with good results)?

# Explicit and Implicit Messages

What we say, don't say, or our facial expressions and voice tone send strong messages to our students. We need to help each other monitor the message(s) our students are receiving.

**Things to think about when reading this story:**

- As you read this story, can you relate to it personally?
- Have you ever worked with a student, colleague or parent who was similar?
- What messages did you send to that student, colleague, or parent verbally or non-verbally?
- How do you believe they remember you?
- How would you like to be remembered by them?
- What did you do to make their life better?
- What did you do that might not have made their life better?

### Explicit and Implicit Messages

The week before the winter holiday is always a tough week, and yesterday we had several kids having a very tough day. I spent some time with three of the kids who were having the toughest of days.

In the conversation with one of these kids, she said something that was just heartbreaking. She said that she had behaved the way she had behaved because, "I am a bad girl." This wasn't something said lightly by her, she really meant it. Her behaviors are not who she is as a person. Her behaviors really were bad behaviors, but she is not a "bad girl."

It is so critically important that we help her, and all children feeling like this, to see the difference. In talking with her, it was clear that she does not believe that she has control over these bad behaviors, given that she is "a bad girl." Until she sees the difference between behavior and person, she will struggle to understand she controls her behaviors.

We, as educators are good, caring, and loving people. We never would explicitly tell a child they are "bad." The problem is that they will read our frustration (frustration that is valid) to mean they *are* bad. This can be in our voices, this can be in our faces, and this can be in our posture. This is the implicit message. This is natural, given what they are doing at that moment is frustrating.

To counteract this, we must be explicit in the messages that we give all children. We must make sure that we tell them clearly the message we want them to have. We must tell them, "I do not like it when you _____, but I do like you. Your behavior does not define you. You can control your behavior. If today was a bad day, because you struggled to control your behavior, tomorrow is a new day and you can be successful."

These are tough days for us and for our kids. Thankfully, we have a break coming up. Thanks for "listening."

**Reflection:**

Now that you have read the story and thought about the questions, it is time to reflect.

- What did you think about when you read this story?
- How can that help you in dealing with current and future students?
- How can that help you in dealing with current and future parents?
- How can that help you in dealing with current and future colleagues?
- What can you do differently starting today, to achieve better results (even if you started with good results)?

# What If You Expect….

At times, we allow "what we expect" to impact our ability to see what is actually occurring or what can or could occur. We need to examine our expectations and see whether or not they are limiting our thinking.

**Things to think about when reading this story:**

- As you read this story, can you relate to it personally?
- Have you ever worked with a student, colleague or parent who was similar?
- What messages did you send to that student, colleague, or parent verbally or non-verbally?
- How do you believe they remember you?
- How would you like to be remembered by them?
- What did you do to make their life better?
- What did you do that might not have made their life better?

**What If You Expect...**

Do you think a 7-year-old, who has lived in the U.S. for only one year and who is still learning English, could qualify for a gifted or highly-capable program? What if that child is writing poetry in their new language?

What if you expect something to occur or be a certain way, and it does not turn out that way? Are you ready, willing and able to learn new perspectives as the situation, what was feared, is playing its way out in your world?

Several years ago, while working on disproportionality issues, I created a way in which to look at our language learners for the possibility of qualification for gifted and highly capable programs. In a nutshell, we used rapid language acquisition to create a pool of students who we then examined to a greater degree. For example, if a student was to go from the bottom 25% of the scores for ELL students in their grade level to the top 25% of the scores for the students in their grade level from one year to the next, they would be chosen for this "pool" of students to examine further.

The reason why this was not used as a determining factor, but instead to create a pool, is that some of the students who do this actually had English language skills that they were not ready/able to demonstrate one year and acculturation allowed them to demonstrate these skills the following year.

Then, we examined the students within this pool of students regarding their rate of growth on reading and math examinations. In a district with roughly 28,000 students, of which roughly 5,800 are ELL qualified students, this pool was about 25-30 kids per grade level examined. When looking at the reading and math scores, we were looking for students who went from very low scores to rather high scores within this same period of time. Within the pool of 25-30 students, we usually found 5-10 students per grade level who made outstanding growth in reading and/or math. These 5-10 students were then found eligible for gifted/highly capable services.

This led to us quadrupling the number of ELL students who were being identified for gifted/highly capable services. These students were qualified in addition to students who qualified via the standard method that only looked at certain tests scores in the same way, regardless of ELL status or not.

The first year that this occurred, the teachers were very apprehensive regarding this significant increase in ELL students within the gifted/highly capable programs. This was a huge change for everyone involved, and change is scary!!! There was a common concern, "How are these students going to keep up? Their English is not strong enough for this program!" They did not expect to have students in their classroom who might (and did) struggle with the English language skills. The administrator who was overseeing the program at the time was, unbeknownst to staff, tracking all of these students and made it very clear that these students needed the services that gifted/highly capable programs had to offer. The administrator, myself, and maybe one or two other people were the only people to know which of the ELL students were placed into the program based upon meeting the same criteria as all other students versus meeting the new criteria. At the end of the school year, there was no difference between the two groups regarding the rate of success. It was the same rate of success for the native English-speaking group.

The teachers demonstrated the ability to adapt to a situation even though their fears and hesitation were telling them it was a bad idea. Change, especially significant change, is often seen as a bad idea. They learned from this situation that these students can be successful, even if there are times in which some extra work needed to occur, like native language support, in order to ensure success.

In our jobs, and our lives, we are often faced with situations in which we do not believe something is going to work. The trick is being willing and able to adapt, being willing and able to keep an open mind, being willing and able to allow new learning to replace old thinking.

Also, this is an example of thinking outside the box in order to fix a problem. This new methodology was very different than what was done before. What was done before this, and sadly is occurring again, led to disproportionate results. If our results are poor, we need to try new ideas and new methods.

**Reflection:**

Now that you have read the story and thought about the questions, it is time to reflect.

- What did you think about when you read this story?
- How can that help you in dealing with current and future students?
- How can that help you in dealing with current and future parents?
- How can that help you in dealing with current and future colleagues?
- What can you do differently starting today, to achieve better results (even if you started with good results)?

# Communication and Relationships

Our ability to communicate with others could be impacted as much or more by our relationship with the other individual than by what is actually being said. How we interpret the message from someone we trust can be totally different than how we interpret the exact same message from someone we do not have a positive/developed relationship with, even when the words are identical.

**Things to think about when reading this story:**

- As you read this story, can you relate to it personally?
- Have you ever worked with a student, colleague or parent who was similar?
- What messages did you send to that student, colleague, or parent verbally or non-verbally?
- How do you believe they remember you?
- How would you like to be remembered by them?
- What did you do to make their life better?
- What did you do that might not have made their life better?

## Communication and Relationships

After spending 8 years as the person that is at times between 100+ staff members and 4 administrators, I have come to have some strong beliefs regarding communication and relationships. I am not one of the administrators, yet my supervisor is the supervisor of the other administrators. I am not a supervisor for the 100+ staff members, yet I coach them every day on what and how they are to complete their jobs.

Through these years, I have learned that the communication within and between these groups is very similar to the communication between children and adults. A question for the reader: What is the difference between children and adults?????

On average, adults are bigger….

As the adults in the educational setting, we are expected to not have the kinds of struggles our students have, and it is likely that this expectation just does not hold any water. Even though we are the adults, we need to develop and maintain relationships in order to be successful in our work. A strange thing about communication is that we can hear the exact same message, word for word, from a friend or trusted source and have no problem with the message. In contrast, if we heard it from someone who is not a friend or is not trusted, we would have a problem.

A school psychologist recently called me to express their significant dislike for one of our administrative staff members. The thing that made her the most upset was that the administrator asked her, "Why are you involved with ….?" Hearing this had a big impact on me, because I ask people that exact same question every single day. After talking with a trusted friend, I realized that this psychologist was so upset because they already had a poor relationship with this administrator. And, they felt that the administrator was not asking the question to understand the involvement, but instead to question the involvement. When I ask the question, I am seeking to understand. Therefore, the exact same words have totally different meaning due to both the relationship I have with the individuals and probably the tone of voice, both of which define the underlying meaning of the question.

Communication relies only in part on the words that are said. People and research talk about a large percentage of a message being non-verbal. I just don't buy that idea. I believe communication relies in part on what is being said, in part on the non-verbal cues, and, in large part, on the trust you have in the person who is speaking.

A principal I once worked with had a saying that I believe covers both our relationships with students and our relationships with other adults in education, "They don't care how much you know until they know how much you care!" The following might also be true--- "They don't care how much authority you have until they know how much you care."

In our work, there is not enough time to do everything perfectly. Therefore, each and every minute that is spent on relationship building and building trust can translate into several hours saved on trying to communicate a message for the third, or fourth, or fifth time that just seems to keep failing. As a leader, the ability to "use" authority is greatly enhanced by the amount of time and effort that went into building a relationship before you need to exercise your authority. As a person who is not in an administrative position, the likelihood of seeking to understand "the boss" when they provide a directive tends to hinge on whether or not you trust the person who has provided the directive.

In this process, both sides have responsibility. Having spent these years in a leadership role without power/authority, I have had to learn many lessons. And, I often learn lessons the hard way (first making mistakes and then having to clean them up). I often see the struggles that both sides are going through. There are times in which people receive directives that they do not like, yet if there is a strong relationship in place they are able to contact the person and seek to understand why the decision was made. There are times in which administrators are given "marching orders" and they do not particularly like what is occurring either.

In the end, in order to have effective communication, both sides need to work to build and maintain relationships. Our administrators need to take the extra minutes to make personal contact when they know they will be asking someone to do something that they might not want to do. Our staff members need to first seek to understand where the administrator is coming from, before seeking to be understood.

These efforts will not solve all of the problems we face, but can lead to building relationships and reducing the time that is taken when communication fails, and therefore, solving some of the problems we face. We are not going to agree 100% of the time, but we can seek to understand and communicate effectively 100% of the time.

**Reflection:**

Now that you have read the story and thought about the questions, it is time to reflect.

- What did you think about when you read this story?
- How can that help you in dealing with current and future students?
- How can that help you in dealing with current and future parents?
- How can that help you in dealing with current and future colleagues?
- What can you do differently starting today, to achieve better results (even if you started with good results)?

### After writing this story:

During the editing phase of this book, the author received a phone call from someone who was very upset with one of the district administrators. They talked about how the person had been asked a question by their school team, and that this person had given them the wrong answer. We talked for a while, and I gave them what I believed to be the correct answer (I was writing the legal and implementation documents for the district at that time). They then told me that the administrator had even sent them an email with his/her response. I asked them to forward me the email and I read it.

To my shock, their answer was almost word-for-word what I had told the team. I asked this person to re-read the email while I waited on the phone. Then, I asked them how it differed from the answer I had provided. They, then, were also shocked. They admitted that the two answers, in all the important factors, were the same answer.

We then had a fascinating talk about how the team doesn't trust, nor like, this administrator. I had heard the same comments from many staff across the district regarding this particular person, so it appeared their feelings were valid. Please note, valid or not, the impact can exist. Nevertheless, I needed to work with the team regarding how their feelings were negatively impacting their ability to hear what this person was saying. In the end, they worked hard to make sure their feelings were not restricting their ability to hear what this person was actually saying.

## What Really Is Important?

We do a lot of work on behalf of our students, yet how often do we think about what is really important to them? What they value? This is a heartwarming story about what was important to a little boy with cerebral palsy.

**Things to think about when reading this story:**

- As you read this story, can you relate to it personally?
- Have you ever worked with a student, colleague or parent who was similar?
- What messages did you send to that student, colleague, or parent verbally or non-verbally?
- How do you believe they remember you?
- How would you like to be remembered by them?
- What did you do to make their life better?
- What did you do that might not have made their life better?

## What Really Is Important?

How 'bout- "What is really important when you are 10 years old and are dealing with cerebral palsy?"

Joe was a 5th grader in an elementary school I worked at. He was born with cerebral palsy that had a significant impact on his daily life. His speech was very 'breathy' and most of us had trouble understanding him. His writing was so poor that it was illegible and he could not walk without the support of a walker. His IEP addressed all three of these areas. Academically, Joe was fine. Cognitively, Joe was fine, but moving around, speaking and writing were all problematic. Joe's goal was not to have a 4.0 (though he did). Joe's goal was not the 'fixing' of his disability or the dream of walking without support. This seemed to be the goal of all the adults in his life, however, Joe's goal was to be able to play soccer for the school team. His friends got to play soccer. They got to wear their uniforms to school and talk about the last game or the upcoming game against another elementary school.

There was one major problem: that walker! The rule, as handed down by the national soccer governing office, FIFA, is that nothing metallic could be on the soccer field, as it would represent potential injury to self or others. The walker was not to be on the field under any circumstance. I even explored changing the game rules when Joe took the field, so that danger to others might be minimal (nobody runs for a period of 3 minutes). FIFA would have nothing to do with such modifications. The walker could not be on the field-end of story.

One night I had a flash- what if Joe were to play goalkeeper on his knees? He was all for it as it meant he would get to play. FIFA had no objection. The school's attorney had no objection. We were all set. Game day saw Joe in the goal on his knees. The game started and you can hear him squeal with delight a mile away. As is often the case though, the best laid plans…..

You see, Joe only could maintain his balance using his hands to hold his body up. He couldn't simply play keeper on his knees; his hands were used to balance him. That left no limbs to stop a shot. Luckily, for most of the game, his defenders protected him, not allowing a single shot on goal. Then the other team broke through the defense and took a shot at goal- dead on. There was a collective gasp from the sideline, the players and the referee as the ball hit Joe square in the face. There was no way for him to avoid it or block it.

Of course, the game was stopped as we all huddled around him. And his response, despite a pretty significant nose bleed, "I stopped the shot." The smile would humble the Cheshire Cat.

We tend to think that the evaluation and IEP is the 'be all, end all' and that it's all about disability; and that our job is to facilitate the whole process. To Joe, a 10-yr old with all sorts of disabilities and significant impacts, it was all about playing a soccer game with friends and representing his school. I helped make that happen and that is what I'll remember long after I retire.

**Reflection:**

Now that you have read the story and thought about the questions, it is time to reflect.

- What did you think about when you read this story?
- How can that help you in dealing with current and future students?
- How can that help you in dealing with current and future parents?
- How can that help you in dealing with current and future colleagues?
- What can you do differently starting today, to achieve better results (even if you started with good results)?

**After writing this story:**

Special education was formalized in 1975 with the passing of federal law 95-142. This, in essence, was the law that guaranteed children with disabilities access to the school building, no matter how severe their disability. But, it really did start out as primarily just access. These children were often separated by putting them away from the other children, even in portables "if necessary."

Over time, special education has changed greatly. One of the major goals at this time is for our children with disabilities to have better post school outcomes. This, in large part, is due to our data indicating that the vast majority of our children with disabilities are not employed nor seeking higher education following graduation from our schools. As a system, we need to make sure that our education and focus for our children with disabilities needs to improve the likelihood that they will have better post K-12 outcomes. We need to make sure that what we emphasize in their IEPs and services is what will be important to them, will lead to better post school outcomes, will lead to success for them.

## Slow Down to Speed Up

Sometimes we want problems to be solved quickly, given the stressors we face. However, there are times in which slowing down, taking extra time in that moment, will save us a great deal of time in the long run. Also, there is a good chance that this can lead to better long-term relationships.

**Things to think about when reading this story:**

- As you read this story, can you relate to it personally?
- Have you ever worked with a student, colleague or parent who was similar?
- What messages did you send to that student, colleague, or parent verbally or non-verbally?
- How do you believe they remember you?
- How would you like to be remembered by them?
- What did you do to make their life better?
- What did you do that might not have made their life better?

## Slow Down to Speed Up

I have spent my career working with kids with emotional or behavioral disabilities and/or behavioral challenges.

Early on I showed promise working with these students, so I got more time working with them. Weird how the world works that way. The better I became at working with these students, the more work I tended to have, and the more pressure.

The pressure came from the expectation I had of myself, and others had of me, that I could enter into any situation and solve it. Early in my career, if needed, I would stop a situation using physical means if necessary. This wasn't often and it wasn't my preference, but I was good at that and the kids knew that I could go "there" if needed. However, with age, even if I lacked wisdom, I was slower and more likely to get injured. This idea of physically responding was taking a back seat to understanding and learning.

With time, I learned that slowing down a little could actually be much faster. Taking a few extra seconds, or even minutes, could save a great deal of time on the "other" end of the process. Also, it tended to build much stronger relationships with the kids. Instead of the kids knowing that, if things became physical, they would lose, the kids learned that I was going to try to understand their perspective and treat them with respect, no matter what had already occurred. I had done the same earlier in my career, but the physical side of things sometimes overshadowed this approach.

This simply occurred by slowing down a little. But, to get to that point, I had to let go of my ego and expectations. Although others still expected things to be solved fast, they eventually learned that "done well" beats "fast" by a mile.

Last year, a student was having meltdowns every single week in the classroom. The first time that I was sent to get him "out of that classroom" I took a lot of time. He was lying curled up on the ground crying. Instead of telling him what he needed to do and instead of telling him what he was doing wrong, I just sat next to him and started to visit about something totally unrelated. Eventually he responded, and we went off to my office. I saw this student almost every single week. Sometimes he would come with me right away, and sometimes not. Either way, when we got to my office, he just played with toys for a few minutes and I faked like there was something important to respond to on my computer. Once his body language had changed, I asked him if he wanted to play some kind of a game and he always did. During the game, in a really low-keyed manner, I asked him about what had occurred. He always gave an accurate description of the events. The problem was that if he was not ready to deal with a problem he had a meltdown. We talked about strategies and he did a great job discussing them.

Now, a year later, his maturity has increased a great deal and he is employing those strategies on a regular basis. Also, 14 weeks into the school year and there has been just one meltdown. The principal did a great job of taking time with this student, since I was gone.

Is it feasible for a classroom teacher to do this? Some days yes and some days no. Luckily, we have a team of people. Also, the amount of time taken by slowing down really does add up to less time over the course of a year (or a couple of years). In this case, the parents dearly love us for the efforts we put in with their child. Due to this trust, we don't have to have long meetings to discuss what has occurred. Each of the problems that occurred, no matter the approach, would have taken some time to resolve. However, that 10-20% more time we took by slowing down was, and is, way less than the combination of saved time from those potential meetings. We saved time by building a relationship with this boy that led to the behaviors virtually disappearing.

What if we had done a special education evaluation? An initial evaluation is 12-20 hours of work. Then, the work of the IEP process. Then, maybe a FBA and BIP. That might have added up to 30-40 hours of work. How many times have you seen an initial evaluation, an FBA, a BIP, and maybe even services in a behavioral classroom lead to a student no longer having meltdowns the following year?

So, will this always work? Probably not. Will it always feel like the right thing to do for the student? Probably yes. And, there is a very good chance that the numbers are on your side. Not only will you probably save time, you will probably lead to better outcomes for kids, and you will probably feel like a more productive professional.

**Reflection:**

Now that you have read the story and thought about the questions, it is time to reflect.

- What did you think about when you read this story?
- How can that help you in dealing with current and future students?
- How can that help you in dealing with current and future parents?
- How can that help you in dealing with current and future colleagues?
- What can you do differently starting today, to achieve better results (even if you started with good results)?

# If Something Goes Wrong, Look Within….

We control our actions and influence the actions of others. If we work exceptionally hard to be introspective and find the ways in which we can improve, allowing ourselves to learn from difficult situations, our long-term outcomes will keep improving.

**Things to think about when reading this story:**

- As you read this story, can you relate to it personally?
- Have you ever worked with a student, colleague or parent who was similar?
- What messages did you send to that student, colleague, or parent verbally or non-verbally?
- How do you believe they remember you?
- How would you like to be remembered by them?
- What did you do to make their life better?
- What did you do that might not have made their life better?

### If Something Goes Wrong, Look Within…

For years now, I have been working with a group of an average of 100 professionals. My role in this group is coaching as well as to take over certain difficult situations and help the group and parents find viable solutions. During these times, I often hear about how the "other person" is bad, evil, mentally ill, crazy, etc… This occurs on both sides in many cases. In the years of doing this work, I have yet to see these feelings and/or thoughts lead to any solutions.

A couple of years ago, I was sitting in a meeting of administrators. The topic was about how frustrated some staff were with regards to the leadership team. During this meeting, one of the newer administrators took the floor and expressed to their workers (and in front of all of us) how it is "them" and not "us" when someone calls and is angry. They went on with this "them" versus "us" discussion for several minutes. I don't know if I was tired that day, but I actually got a bit angry and confrontational. I was so concerned that the message being given was going to lead to even worse relationships and also lead to zero problems being solved, so I spoke my mind that morning.

I had interesting responses from the group: The supervisor of that administrator was very happy with my thoughts and comments. Also, one of the direct reports (i.e., workers who are under the supervision of the administrator) of the administrator who suggested not taking personal responsibility started coming to me for mentoring. In contrast, the administrator who suggested not taking personal responsibility never said a single word to me.

In working with my group, and especially during 1-to-1 coaching, I work very hard with people to talk about introspection being the first step when there is a problem or a failed interaction. That is, the first questions should be: 1) What could I have done better? 2) What could I have done differently in order to have achieved a different (better) result? In 99.9 percent of the cases, we will find that we could have done something better or differently. Is it possible that our actions would have solved the problem that occurred? Maybe. It is also possible that they might not have.

The key to this approach is that we approach each situation with a desire to understand and to learn. This will make us better over time because of what we learn. Also, if we realize that we have goofed up a situation, and we have the courage to truly analyze our own behavior, we might just have the opportunity to make things better quickly. That is, we can approach the other person, or the group, and say, "I goofed, I should have said or done _____." There is tremendous power in approaching other people and being honest about making a mistake and actually naming and owning our mistake(s).

This problem of not taking ownership is magnified at times by our extensive usage of email as a form of communication. In email, we lack the non-verbal cues and social language cues that are sometimes needed to both express and understand the messages that are critical to ensure that there is true understanding.

Recently I needed specific information from individuals in the group in order to purchase materials that they needed for their work. If I had asked them about the materials in a group setting, the facial expressions and the quick whisper to a neighbor would have told me that I had not been clear enough in my message. I could have asked follow-up questions until we as a group were on the same page. Instead, because there was a rush to get the order placed, I tried to get this information over email. This was a major mistake. The vocabulary that the company uses is very familiar to me. However, nobody else actually works with this company. It took multiple emails and explanations to solve what was really a rather simple problem, all due to a little bit of miscommunication. I made the mistake, and we all paid for the mistake. In the end, not only was I frustrated, but others were also very frustrated. The group, though, was rather forgiving once I explained the error I had made and apologized for my frustration.

During the problem noted above, I was clearly upset with the group for what appeared to be truly random answers. What really helped us to resolve this problem was the questions by staff about: What are you talking about….? This led me to realize that our confusion was caused by my assumption that the terms I was using were meaningful to the group., and only after I remembered that I needed to look at my behaviors and what I could say or do better in the situation. So, even though I have a lot of experience, I still started out on the wrong road.

No matter what training and skills we have, we are all still just people going through our days trying to get our jobs done. We are going to make mistakes. The big question is: how do we respond to our mistakes?

After years of helping young professionals, I have seen this play out multiple times during the development of these young professionals. There have been many cases in which a professional new to the field was showing tremendous promise and potential. Some of these people over the course of their first five years made amazing growth and are growing into leaders within their groups. Some, however, made little or no growth, some have even appeared to go backwards with regards to skills and/or abilities.

In my experience, there is a direct correlation between the people who make strong growth being great at introspection and the people who make little or no growth struggling with introspection. All of these people are smart people, yet introspection is something that requires letting go of ego issues and a willingness to suffer a little pain. It is a little bit painful for someone who is highly successful, highly talented, and very smart, to first look at what they have done wrong. Yet, it is a recipe for strong growth over time. Finally, because this is not meant to be critical, but is meant to be a path to higher levels of success, it is important to keep track of personal growth and progress.

**Reflection:**

Now that you have read the story and thought about the questions, it is time to reflect.

- What did you think about when you read this story?
- How can that help you in dealing with current and future students?
- How can that help you in dealing with current and future parents?
- How can that help you in dealing with current and future colleagues?
- What can you do differently starting today, to achieve better results (even if you started with good results)?

**After writing this story:**

During the editing phase of writing this book, one of the early readers asked for suggestions on how to keep track of personal growth and success.

The first idea is about changing the tape that runs in your head. That is, many high performers will immediately and automatically play down any positive feedback that they receive. Therefore, each person needs to catch themselves during these times and analyze this behavior. If there is someone giving you positive feedback, you need to take the time to think about it, to absorb it, and to take some pride in it.

The second idea is to work with your significant other on this topic. If you are a high performer, it is likely that your annual review will reflect this. It is also likely that you will struggle to read it, hear it, and accept it. You can ask your significant other to read this to you. This will be a painful experience at times, but part of the process of accepting what you have done well.

# It Just Takes One Caring Adult Relationship

The research is clear that each child who is struggling can be greatly impacted by just one adult caring about them (from the perspective of the student, not just the adult). This story describes two children, a brother and a sister, who grew up in the same environment, but had dramatically different results, the successful one showing how certain teachers had such a powerful impact on the child's life. This story is told from the brother's point of view and memory.

**Things to think about when reading this story:**

- As you read this story, can you relate to it personally?
- Have you ever worked with a student, colleague or parent who was similar?
- What messages did you send to that student, colleague, or parent verbally or non-verbally?
- How do you believe they remember you?
- How would you like to be remembered by them?
- What did you do to make their life better?
- What did you do that might not have made their life better?

**It Just Takes One Caring Adult Relationship**

The siblings grew up in the same home until their parents divorced. It was an ugly divorce, and a memory that both siblings have is hearing the parents fight about who would take the kids. Neither parent wanted to take them. They literally argued in front of these two children about who was going to have to take them after the divorce.

These two were quite a mess by this point in time. Both had suffered abuse and neglect, and both were seen as "terrible" kids. By age 14 the sister became a runaway and was living on the streets at about age 16. She later became a drug addict, and her life has continued to be very difficult. The brother struggled in school, and by some dumb luck learned that teachers hated to have a long-haired hippy do well in school.

The boy, however, had two main motivations in school. He had one teacher at each level (elementary, middle and high school) who treated him like a human being, and he was motivated to maintain those relationships. The other motivation was to drive teachers, in general, crazy. As the years progressed, he succeeded at both. He had teachers who asked if he wanted them to visit once he was in prison. He had teachers who asked what kind of flowers he wanted on his grave. Little did they know, that was rather motivating to him. If getting a good grade in their class was enough to get them angry, then "game on."

Almost every new teacher accused him of cheating after the first test, but one teacher took this to a whole other level. After arriving at school in the mornings, the boy was summoned to the assistant principal's office. This occurred so often that they would just do it over the loud speaker to save paper and time.

One morning, he arrived at the assistant principal's office in time to hear the assistant principal and this teacher arguing. The argument was rather simple:

"He cheated…"

"Probably not…"

"He cheated…"

"Have you looked at his cumulative folder?"

"He must have cheated, just look at him. There is no way someone who looks like that could possibly get 100% on one of my tests."

That was just one argument that the brother overheard during his years in school.

Later on, in high school, the boy worked as a TA. That teacher, one of the significant teachers in his life, told him about another argument. In the teachers' lounge the teacher was teased about being stuck with him as a TA. This teacher told the others, "He is the best TA I have ever had, you just have to be nice to him."

The boy had been suspended from every school he had attended (and when he went to college, they threatened to expel him). This is where the importance of the "one significant, caring adult relationship" made the big difference, all the way through college. Over the years, each of these significant adults in this young man's life talked *with* him, and not *at* him. They showed an interest in him, what he was doing, what he liked, what he wanted to be. This made all the difference in keeping him in school. Although he had fun tormenting teachers who treated him poorly, it just was not enough. Also, these people would, because of the relationship they had built with him, help him see the error of certain decisions he had made. These caring adults were the key in him wanting to become a teacher as he became older. His sister, on the other hand, did not experience this kind of support.

This young man went on to college to become a teacher. The main desire was that he would have the opportunity to be that special person in the life of some student, or some students. Today, he is that person who can help children who are struggling when most people either cannot or will not help.

**Reflection:**

- Now that you have read the story and thought about the questions, it is time to reflect.
- What did you think about when you read this story?
- How can that help you in dealing with current and future students?
- How can that help you in dealing with current and future parents?
- How can that help you in dealing with current and future colleagues?
- What can you do differently starting today, to achieve better results (even if you started with good results)?

# Our Language Learners and Special Education

Some groups of our language learners are qualified for special education at much higher rates, and this indicates that many students without disabilities are seen as children with disabilities. This often leads to them not getting the actual services that they need. This story is about some children who were negatively impacted by our system. We are good and caring people, as educators, so these results are unacceptable.

**Things to think about when reading this story:**

- As you read this story, can you relate to it personally?
- Have you ever worked with a student, colleague or parent who was similar?
- What messages did you send to that student, colleague, or parent verbally or non-verbally?
- How do you believe they remember you?
- How would you like to be remembered by them?
- What did you do to make their life better?
- What did you do that might not have made their life better?

## Our Language Learners and Special Education

I happen to be a bilingual school psychologist in a middle to large sized school district. Over the years, I have seen many, many Spanish speaking students qualified for special education or recommended for special education evaluation in complete error. And, these students are not getting the language support that they need to be successful. Here are a few examples.

## "I already know how to read in Spanish"

The first student who I am going to talk about was in high school when I was asked to complete a bilingual evaluation. I was invited by the building school psychologist after this student told her, "I don't know why you people have me in this class, I already know how to read and write in Spanish."

This student came to the United States in the seventh grade and was placed into special education. There was more to the story and the original team didn't get everything wrong; however, nobody looked at what this student could do, only at what he "couldn't do in English." It didn't take long until they moved this student into a self-contained special education classroom. In this classroom, he was working on letter sounds and letter names. The school psychologist was impressed by this young man and his conviction, enough so that she believed he might be telling her the truth regarding his skills. However, she had no way to measure them.

I completed the evaluation, and this student was reading at the 10th grade level in Spanish, and his math was at the highest level in which he had instruction (the 6th grade level). Therefore, he was spending day after day in an environment that was totally inappropriate for him. I wonder what his teachers were thinking along the way? How was it that nobody noticed this? If it were not for his efforts to self-advocate, nobody would have ever known about his skills, just his deficits in a language he had only recently started to learn.

He wants to be a teacher someday.

### Learning disability in one language and not the other?

This little boy was in the second grade in a bilingual education school. The school psychologist invited me in to complete core academic testing with this student. The teachers were convinced that he had a learning disability. The testing showed his core academic skills, when testing was completed in Spanish, were at the third-grade level. Still, the teachers struggled to believe that he didn't have a learning disability. It would be pretty darn hard to have a learning disability in one language and not the other.

### No formal education

In this example, the student was already qualified for special education and the school psychologist wanted to see how he would perform if tested in his native language. This student stated that he did not know how to read in Spanish, and he had no formal education in Spanish. The school psychologist had tested numerous students who have said the same thing, and the norm is that they try to read the Spanish as though it is English. However, this student demonstrated early reading skills in Spanish. If it were not for learned helplessness that he demonstrated at school and in the testing, it is likely that he would have performed at the mid-second grade level in reading in Spanish.

I began the intelligence testing in Spanish. He performed in the average range on the subtests that did not require verbal comprehension as part of the response. The testing showed that he did not have strong enough vocabulary in Spanish to be able to perform in Spanish on an IQ test. This is pretty common, if a student has not received formal education in their native language and/or is not literate in their native language.

Stephen Krashen, a leading expert in language acquisition, states that our higher-level vocabulary and language structures develop through reading. So, I went on to test this student in receptive and expressive vocabulary using a test that is designed to be a Spanish-English Bilingual test. He scored well below the average for vocabulary, which again, was what was expected (i.e., he didn't have the exposure, nor the experience needed to develop these skills in both languages). He needed to work on core vocabulary in both languages in order to have a high likelihood of success.

I talked to the student about how I learned to speak Spanish using the recommendations of Stephen Krashen. It is all about comprehensible input, which can occur via reading books at your level and moving upward with success. The student came back the following day and told me that he had told his mother about this idea, and she sent him straight to the library to get books in Spanish. This student has a huge desire to learn, and his parents have a huge desire for him to learn and be successful. They just needed ideas regarding what will help him to make better progress.

### He doesn't speak that language

This last example might be the most unusual, strange, sad case that I have seen. I was a lead for the school psychologists when I got a call from one of the school psychologists in a little bit of a panic. There was a student who had enrolled and the paperwork indicated that he needed a self-contained special education setting for students with severe disabilities. The school psychologist met the student, and the boy didn't present like this at all. Students who need a restrictive placement such as this usually struggle with communication skills (in general, not language learning) and social skills, and this student didn't present this way.

The school psychologist went on to get an interpreter, to try to get to the bottom of this mystery. The previous school district had evaluated this student after 2 months into the country. They found him to have a severe intellectual disability and to be in need of this type of placement. Sadly, they had made a large error and a huge error.

First, this student (an eighth grader when he arrived in our district 18 months later) had never been in school before. Second, as a child moving to California from Mexico, the school assumed that he spoke Spanish. So, all interactions with him had been in Spanish (leading to the special education evaluation). Also, the special education evaluation was all done in Spanish. However, he did not speak nor understand a single word of Spanish. Imagine how you would do if evaluated in a language in which you did not understand a single word.

We ended up having to "punt" in this situation. There was no program that was right for him, but we knew for sure a self-contained special education program placement for a student who presented as cognitively normal was not the right decision. We created a truly one-off program for him in his school. Sadly, he moved sixth months later. We were able to right one wrong, but I don't know if we got him far enough along the right path with our work.

Evaluating language learners for special education services is a very difficult task to do correctly. Also, we have a lot of disproportionality within our language learners, and it is mostly over qualification of certain student groups within certain disability categories. It is clear that we need to do a better job, and each and every one of us needs to look at language learners first with a lens of what they can do. This will help us better understand the meaning of the skills they are not yet demonstrating.

**Reflection:**

Now that you have read the story and thought about the questions, it is time to reflect.

- What did you think about when you read this story?
- How can that help you in dealing with current and future students?
- How can that help you in dealing with current and future parents?
- How can that help you in dealing with current and future colleagues?
- What can you do differently starting today, to achieve better results (even if you started with good results)?

# Boys and Girls: What are we reinforcing?

This story talks about how our behaviors are probably reinforcing some of the gender stereotypes (and other things too) that could cause our children and students problems as they become adults. Also, it is likely that most people are unaware of their acculturated behaviors in this area (and other areas, too).

**Things to think about when reading this story:**

- As you read this story, can you relate to it personally?
- Have you ever worked with a student, colleague or parent who was similar?
- What messages did you send to that student, colleague, or parent verbally or non-verbally?
- How do you believe they remember you?
- How would you like to be remembered by them?
- What did you do to make their life better?
- What did you do that might not have made their life better?

**Boys and Girls: are we reinforcing what we want to reinforce….**

I am about 25 years into my educational career, and I am watching what is going on in our country with men and women, and wondering if some of this starts with us, those of us raising kids and working with kids.

We still think it is ok for a girl to cry when they are upset, but not so ok for a boy to cry when they are upset. We still talk about girl colors and boy colors. And, it goes a lot deeper than this!

Personally, I had a tragic event in my life that showed me how extremely different men and women can and do get treated when a tragedy occurs. One of my children, a little girl, died. At that same time, I had just started graduate school in psychology. So, I was thinking a lot about emotions and how people are treated, and how people react. After my daughter died, virtually everyone asked me how my wife was doing. I could count on one hand, with fingers left over, how many people asked me how I was doing. Men are supposed to be tough, stoic, take care of their woman….. blah, blah, blah…. But my daughter's death is something that impacted the remainder of my life, luckily in some ways that have been rather positive.

Why do we still treat boys and girls so differently? Is there any logic to this?

What does not make sense is treating boys and girls differently and then expecting that there will be no long-term problems associated with this. Our society still struggles to see women as mathematicians or engineers, and our society still struggles to see men as "stay home" parents or nurses.

Take a couple of weeks, watch the commercials on television and think about the differences. For example, how many times will there be commercials about men trying to do something within the home and totally ruining it (and never the reverse)?

How many times will there be commercials about woman receiving jewelry from men (and never the reverse)?

We have expectations of how boys are supposed to be and how girls are supposed to be, and we start this during parenting of our children and carry it on during the schooling of our children. The problem is that this occurs for about 20 years, then these children are supposed to be men and women. What if, subtly or not so subtly, we create and reinforce expectations of behavior? Then, what if all of the "new" generation suddenly starts to see these roles and behaviors differently.

Have you ever thought about how you interact with children when you first meet them? Oftentimes I catch myself commenting on the clothing that a little girl is wearing, "I like your sparkly shoes" as a way to start a conversation with her. But when I first meet a young boy, I very rarely comment on his appearance, and choose to break the ice with a question about his favorite things (assuming sports and cars for boys...). This may subtly reinforce to girls that I'm paying to attention to their appearance. Could this have something to do with why eating disorders are on the rise, and plastic surgery is advertised on the radio and TV?

It is reasonable to assume that at some point in the past the roles of men and women really didn't change that much from one generation to the next. It is also reasonable to assert that the past 2-3 generations have seen major changes in roles of men and women.

So, what is occurring in our households and our schools that will impact our children, 15 to 20 years from now? Are we thinking about the ways in which we reinforce certain behaviors that are "boy" behaviors and certain behaviors that are "girl" behaviors? How will this impact the next generations?

In the end, we need to make sure that we reinforce in our children the beliefs that we want them to have as they become adults Yet, we also need to consider whether or not what we currently believe is actually good for these soon to be adults

Reinforcing these norms is a very subtle process, so don't think you have "escaped this" unless you have given this true reflection time and asked a trusted individual to process this with you. We are all very good at living in denial and "escaping" through inaction. We need to act, to change our behavior.

**Reflection:**

Now that you have read the story and thought about the questions, it is time to reflect.

- What did you think about when you read this story?
- How can that help you in dealing with current and future students?
- How can that help you in dealing with current and future parents?
- How can that help you in dealing with current and future colleagues?
- What can you do differently starting today, to achieve better results (even if you started with good results)?

**After writing this story:**

During the editing of this book, one of the readers helped the authors to see that this story might already be outdated or limiting, yet still very valuable. That is, it is possible that by the time the next generation becomes adults, there might not be common usage of the words "girls," "boys," "men," or "women." It is possible that this binary system will no longer exist. Therefore, are we even thinking about this when we work with our children? Has this entered into our thoughts when we think about the impact of the language we use with children? What we reinforce? This is an area the reader should, as a lifelong learner and educator of children, read about and think about.

# A Parent's Journey Through Having Their Child Evaluated

This is the story of a person who works within the field of special education and how the process of a special education referral and evaluation for their own child felt to them. It is oftentimes very difficult to help people understand the extreme feelings a parent goes through during this process (which is why it is so critical to KNOW that a referral is the right thing to do, in place of "thinking" it).

**Things to think about when reading this story:**

- As you read this story, can you relate to it personally?
- Have you ever worked with a student, colleague or parent who was similar?
- What messages did you send to that student, colleague, or parent verbally or non-verbally?
- How do you believe they remember you?
- How would you like to be remembered by them?
- What did you do to make their life better?
- What did you do that might not have made their life better?

**A Parent's Journey Through Having Their Child Evaluated**

She was born promptly on her due date. Everything about our sweet baby Katelyn happened right on time, meeting all of her early developmental milestones like sitting up, babbling, and first words. As a pediatric speech language pathologist, I found comfort and pride in knowing that my perfect baby was developing normally. While my training taught me that typical child development occurs naturally, I felt like I must be doing something right as a mother because my little one was blossoming.

As Katelyn approached 8 months, I started preparing for the next developmental milestone – crawling! I baby proofed the house and placed toys just out of her reach during tummy time to encourage her to crawl. At 9 months, she learned how to shift from a sitting position onto her hands and knees. "This is it!" I thought, "She's ready to crawl." As she approached 10 months and made no further progress in crawling, I assured myself that her motor development had paused due to significant development in her language skills that month. Katelyn turned 11 months and created the quirkiest way of moving around the room. She would lie on her back and use her heels to push herself headward until she was next to a toy, then barrel roll over and over sideways until she could reach it.

Even without formal training in motor development, I knew something wasn't right. "I haven't spent enough time working on crawling with her. From now on, every evening we're going to work on crawling," I told myself. "Maybe if she sees me crawl, then she'll be motivated to try harder to crawl." I crawled on the floor until my knees hurt. Her father and I worked together to move her through the crawling movements – one of us holding her up on her hands and knees and the other moving her arms and legs forward. "Maybe this is normal crawling development?"

I wondered. I was scared to admit to myself that something might be wrong with my baby.

I went to a Seattle Sounders soccer game with a friend who worked as a speech language pathologist in an Early Intervention clinic, providing therapy services for children from birth to three years. For most of the game, we chatted about work, life, and family. Throughout our conversation, I struggled with whether or not to ask her about Katelyn's crawling. I knew as soon as I uttered the words, Pandora's box would be open and there was no more pretending that Katelyn was fine and developing normally. I finally worked up the nerve to ask her opinion. After hearing how Katelyn was sliding and rolling around the floor, and asking some follow-up questions, my friend gently said an evaluation might be a good idea. I can still vividly picture that moment and feel the knot in my stomach when I was forced to accept that something might be wrong.

I scheduled an evaluation through the Early Intervention clinic. Driving to the appointment, I held on to hope that they would tell me my perfect baby was developing normally and I had nothing to worry about. At one point during the drive, the butterflies in my stomach were so strong that I nearly turned the car around and canceled the appointment. After parking at the clinic, I sat in the car for a moment, feeling heavy with the thought that within an hour, I might learn that something is wrong with my baby.

In my work as a speech language pathologist, conducting evaluations is part of my job. I knew what to expect in terms of the evaluation process – I would answer questions about Katelyn's development, they would ask her to complete some activities, and they would scrutinize every movement she made. I was worried that I might answer a question incorrectly or Katelyn might not perform. It was intimidating to know that clinical decisions about my child would be made after knowing her for less than an hour.

The evaluation team was made up of more people than I'd expected. Looking back now, it was probably only four or five people, but at the time, it felt like the entire office came to examine every aspect of Katelyn's development. The evaluation went by quickly. Katelyn was charming and engaging, stacking the blocks they gave to her, pointing to the pictures they said, and saying the few words she knew. As they began the motor assessment, my heart sank. She couldn't transition from lying down to sitting up without struggling, she couldn't hold her head up against gravity when they lifted her in the air, and she couldn't crawl to the toys they held out of her reach. I'd seen small indications of motor difficulty at home but it was hard to see her fail so many skills in just five minutes. I kept silently willing her to be stronger and pass the evaluation tasks, but she struggled with one activity after another.

After finishing the evaluation, the team left the room to write a brief summary of their assessment. Finding myself alone with Katelyn, I struggled to fight back tears. I'd seen her fail the assessment tasks and I knew without a doubt that something was wrong. She happily played with the toys in the room while my mind and heart raced. Twenty minutes later, one of the evaluators came back into the room and told me that Katelyn qualified for Early Intervention services to address her motor delay.

I stopped listening after I heard those words. I had initiated the evaluation. I knew she wasn't crawling. But I had held out hope that I was wrong and the evaluation team would tell me that my perfect baby was developing normally and I had nothing to worry about. I worked hard to smile and not cry as the evaluator summarized their findings. She told me the full report would come in the mail within a week and I drove home. Two scripts ran simultaneously though my head while I drove home – "It's just a motor delay. It's not that big of a deal. There are plenty of children who have much more serious problems. This is why Early Intervention exists, so Katelyn can receive therapy services and be just fine when she grows up." Those positive, glass-half-full thoughts were overshadowed by fear and anger, "This isn't fair! Why can't my baby crawl when others figure it out without any problems? What did I do to cause this? Should I not have eaten that one turkey sandwich while I was pregnant? Did I not do enough tummy time with her when she was younger? Is she ever going to walk? Will she be able to play on the playground with the other kids?"

A week later the full evaluation report arrived in the mail. I skimmed through the report, jumping ahead to the motor section. I cried as soon as I saw the motor evaluation heading: standard score = 70, standard deviation: -2.0. I work with standard scores and standard deviations for a living. I know that a standard score of 85 is ok, 77 is worrisome, and 70 is bad news. How could my perfect baby have a standard score of 70? Katelyn's motor delays now had a number assigned to them and the number wasn't good. There's no arguing with a number, there's no shred of hope left with a number, and there's no gray area with a number. It was difficult to see her delay quantified.

We began Early Intervention services with the physical therapist coming to our house. It was initially uncomfortable having a stranger in our home, guiding Katelyn through activities that were hard for her and teaching me how to teach Katelyn. In the first few sessions, I didn't understand the purpose of the activities. Why were we having Katelyn sit on the floor and stack blocks? How was that going to help her crawl? I learned to ask questions so I could understand the progression of skills. The physical therapist explained that we were having Katelyn sit on the floor and reach out for the block so she could practice shifting her weight and strengthening her core muscles, which would help her crawl. Slowly I started to understand the purpose behind the activities and slowly Katelyn started to improve. After six months of weekly therapy, Katelyn had progressed past crawling and started walking. The physical therapist said she was ready to exit services and had caught up to her peers. With the support of Early Intervention services, Katelyn outgrew her motor delay.

My experiences as a parent going through the referral, evaluation, and therapy processes have shaped my practice as a speech language pathologist. These are some of the lessons that guide my professional practice, five years after experiencing this as a parent.

- It took me two months of silently worrying about Katelyn's development to reach the point that I could say my concerns aloud to my friend at the Sounders game. Even then, I hadn't yet accepted that something may really be wrong. Accepting that something is "wrong" with your child takes a lot of time, and many of our parents are in the middle of the acceptance process. Even if the parent has initiated the referral, they're probably still holding out some hope that the professional will say there's nothing wrong with their child. While it can be a relief to finally have an answer, it was heartbreaking to hear that my baby had a delay.

- Realize that even if parents maintain their composure during the meeting, they may still be falling apart inside. I cried in private multiple times before, during, and after the evaluation. It's a raw and scary feeling knowing that your child isn't developing normally like other children. While I probably appeared outwardly composed, I couldn't process all the information I was told. I was grateful that the evaluators were kind and gentle with me, gave me written information that I could review at home as I slowly processed everything, and patiently answered questions that I sometimes asked two or three times.

- I wondered for a long time what I did to cause Katelyn's motor delay and if I could've done something different to prevent or treat it. It was a tremendous amount of guilt to think that I might've done something that was making her life harder. Be gentle with parents because they're being hard on themselves.

- Explain what you're doing and why you're doing the therapy activities if parents join the session. As a clinician, it's easy to move through treatment activities when I understand the progression of skills and therapeutic targets. To an untrained parent, the activities all look the same and can appear like a waste of time. As soon as I understood what skill the activity was developing, and what skill would come next, I understood the purpose of therapy.

- My final take-away from my experience was to never underestimate the long-term power of our professions. The speech language pathologist who teaches a child to say "r" is giving him the sounds that he'll someday say during his wedding vows. The occupational therapist who teaches a child handwriting is helping her fill out her first job application. The physical therapist who teaches a child to walk is helping him chase after his future grandchildren. The school psychologist who identifies a need for social-emotional instruction is giving the gift of future late-night gossip sessions with college friends.

As a speech language pathologist, the faces of the many children I've worked with blend together into happy memories. As a parent of a child who received services, the faces of the therapists remain clear in my mind. Katelyn and I may now just be blips on the therapists' radar but they played such a special role in her development that I still vividly remember each of them. Sometimes when I watch her bravely scale the climbing wall at the park or kick a goal during soccer practice, I say a quiet thank you to the team from five years ago, whose knowledge and compassion gave her the skills to continue being successful as she grows.

**Reflection:**

Now that you have read the story and thought about the questions, it is time to reflect.

- What did you think about when you read this story?
- How can that help you in dealing with current and future students?
- How can that help you in dealing with current and future parents?
- How can that help you in dealing with current and future colleagues?
- What can you do differently starting today, to achieve better results (even if you started with good results)?

# Say "Start" Instead of "Stop"

Many children often hear "stop" throughout their day. Some of these children know what they are supposed to stop doing, however, some don't. And, many of these students don't know what they are supposed to *start* doing. This story focuses in on telling students what to start doing, instead of what to stop doing which will likely lead to more success for all involved.

**Things to think about when reading this story:**

- As you read this story, can you relate to it personally?
- Have you ever worked with a student, colleague or parent who was similar?
- What messages did you send to that student, colleague, or parent verbally or non-verbally?
- How do you believe they remember you?
- How would you like to be remembered by them?
- What did you do to make their life better?
- What did you do that might not have made their life better?

## Say "Start" Instead of "Stop"

I was walking through a school today and heard someone yell "Stop that" at a student.

Throughout my career, I have heard about students who just would not do the right thing, and I have always wondered whether or not they knew what the right thing to do was, or whether they could do it, even if they knew it.

Ross Greene is a leading expert in this area and his books are well worth reading. A key concept from his work is, "they would if they could." This isn't only referring to their physical ability to do something. Instead, this is about a student either not knowing the correct action or not having a specific skill in order to do that "right thing" that we keep talking about.

So, instead of us telling kids to stop _____, what if we told them to start _____?

Instead of creating what could be a guessing game for the student, when we say, "stop that" or "you know the right thing to do," we actually said to them, "I would like you to _____."

An argument that I have heard many times over is the following: "I have already taught them the skill x number of times, so they know what to do." Well, they are not doing it. So, either they didn't learn the skill or they cannot perform the skill under pressure. Maybe what we need to do is remind them of our expectations.

There is a student in my current building who has mastered the "zones" training and every other type of training like that (these are trainings meant to help students with social emotional learning and emotional regulation). When calm, she can explain, maybe even teach, every aspect of those different trainings that we have instilled into her young head. However, this darling little girl struggles with anxiety. She has decked a couple of boys in her time here and she has acted in ways in which adults have left the situation needing a little bit of ice on their sore bodies. However, in each and every situation there were warning signs (i.e., she becomes rather agitated prior to any aggression). Then, in each of the cases, she perceived the situation as though she was physically trapped. This analysis resulted from us spending a great deal of time, after she demonstrated aggression, analyzing her actions and reactions during the situation. In working with her on a regular basis, it became rather obvious that she responded well to being asked and responded poorly to being told. And, if she didn't respond well when asked to do something, she tended to respond well when given a second request with another option that the adults could live with.

One day she was highly agitated, and got into a physical altercation with an adult. She was running away from adults, when I simply asked her if she wouldn't mind sitting on the bench with me for a few minutes. She sat on the bench with me, and then eventually explained the situation from her perspective. I didn't ask her to "stop" doing anything, but instead asked her to "start" doing something.

This usually works best when what you ask the student to do competes with what you don't want them doing. I didn't want her running away from adults, and she would not be running if she was sitting down.

In my building, we have had a series of students who cry very loudly. In each of the cases, these students were on the autism spectrum. For many reasons, it is difficult to have a student who cries loudly within a school setting. Asking these students to "stop" crying certainly would not be of much use. Instead, we always work on what they could start doing that might lead to them to stop crying. In some cases, it has been as simple as giving them a stuffed animal that they like to hold. In some of the cases, it has been asking them to show another person the new book they are reading. And, in some of the cases it has been telling them how much we would like to help, but to help we need to be able to understand what they are trying to tell us and that we need them to start speaking in a voice we can understand. We always focus on what they could start doing, instead of what they need to stop doing.

Some people might be right about the student knowing what "the right thing to do is…" However, that approach tends to lead to the student repeating the unwanted behavior over and over. So, whether they know the "right" thing to do or not, taking the approach of asking them or telling them what to start doing is far more likely to lead to positive results.

We as adults often struggle to do what we know is the right thing to do in a situation that is stressful or difficult for us. For our children, the challenges are even greater. We can reduce those challenges by providing them with "what to start doing" in place of what to stop doing. This reinforces the skills we have been trying to teach them and allows them an opportunity to demonstrate those skills even when under stress.

So, please start telling students what it is you would like them to do.

**Reflection:**

Now that you have read the story and thought about the questions, it is time to reflect.

- What did you think about when you read this story?
- How can that help you in dealing with current and future students?
- How can that help you in dealing with current and future parents?
- How can that help you in dealing with current and future colleagues?
- What can you do differently starting today, to achieve better results (even if you started with good results)?

# Just Stop….

We often struggle with something in our own lives, and we almost always know someone who is struggling with something in their life. Often, these struggles have more to do with the internal messages that we are telling ourselves than with reality. Often, we need to stop with negative messages and start with positive internal messages.

If you read the story "Say start instead of stop….," then this will sound like a contradiction. In the end though, it really is about starting and not stopping.

**Things to think about when reading this story:**

- As you read this story, can you relate to it personally?
- Have you ever worked with a student, colleague or parent who was similar?
- What messages did you send to that student, colleague, or parent verbally or non-verbally?
- How do you believe they remember you?
- How would you like to be remembered by them?
- What did you do to make their life better?
- What did you do that might not have made their life better?

## Just Stop…

Lots of people struggle with anxiousness, some even have anxiety. Lots of people get nervous when they have to speak in front of others, take a test, or a myriad of other possibilities. And, sometimes, people need to just stop doing this to themselves.

I have said that to people before, and they tell me, "I can't." The funny part is that they don't even know what they are doing to feed the anxiety and why they are doing it, not at any deep level. In this case, the "it" can be negative self-talk, self-harming behaviors, avoidance of situations or environments, and more. And, a lot of us have fears and anxieties about what we think might happen, often assuming the worst, instead of what really is happening or what is likely to happen. So, if something really is not happening or is extremely unlikely to happen, then why not just stop worrying, stop being nervous, stop being anxious? How about letting go of those feelings that have little or nothing to do with any reality?

I grew up hearing a lot more about what was wrong with me than about what I did well or any abilities I had. By the time I was in high school and all of the way through graduate school, I had an "A" average in school. Not perfect, but pretty darn good. Nevertheless, I was terrified before virtually all important tests. By the time I was in graduate school I had a pattern of behaviors that helped me through this. Before every important test I would arrive about 30 minutes early and talk to myself about my history. I would remind myself how I had done very well in school, and this test was no different. I would tell myself how I had prepared for this test, and that I was going to do well.

I didn't stop having those feelings, but I stopped allowing them to control me or to control the outcome. Most of the people who I have met over the years who are struggling with being nervous or anxious have an internal tape that plays in their head about the situation. That internal tape is all about what is going to go wrong or what could go wrong, about how the person just is not capable.

So, just stop playing that tape in your head. It is highly unlikely that the bad outcome that you are predicting is going to occur. However, a focus on the bad outcome certainly increases the likelihood of it occurring.

If you like to rock climb, ski, whitewater kayak, mountain bike, or race cars you know that you can have a rather poor outcome occur rather quickly, and there is a sure way of creating that outcome. All you have to do is think for a second or two, "I cannot _____." Pretty much the moment you allow yourself to think that, you fall or crash. However, if you visualize yourself making it through whatever the challenge is that you are facing, you have a pretty good chance of success. So, negative thoughts virtually guarantee the negative outcome and positive thoughts give you a reasonable chance of success.

Going back to the tape that is playing in your head. The way you "just stop" playing that tape is by replacing it with a new tape. Think about positive messages that you can provide yourself before and during the stressful situation. Then, success can breed more success. Am I saying that you will suddenly lose all fear and/or anxiety with regards to whatever your struggle is in life? No, I am not. Instead, I am saying that you have an opportunity to no longer allow yourself to be controlled by your fears and/or anxiety. Really, what is the worst thing that can happen if you struggle during some public speaking? What is the worst thing that can happen if you struggle when trying to run a meeting? I am pretty sure in our part of the world nobody loses their life because they need to get better at public speaking or better at leading a meeting.

Give yourself a real chance at success. Just stop, with the negative self-talk. Just start, with a new tape in your head about the things that can and will make you successful.

**Reflection:**

Now that you have read the story and thought about the questions, it is time to reflect.

- What did you think about when you read this story?
- How can that help you in dealing with current and future students?
- How can that help you in dealing with current and future parents?
- How can that help you in dealing with current and future colleagues?
- What can you do differently starting today, to achieve better results (even if you started with good results)?

# Journey Around the World and the Impact of Teachers

This story tells the journey of a young man from his early years in Somalia, to eventually finishing a master's degree here in the United States. Teachers played a critical role and had both positive and negative impacts along the way.

### Things to think about when reading this story:

- As you read this story, can you relate to it personally?
- Have you ever worked with a student, colleague or parent who was similar?
- What messages did you send to that student, colleague, or parent verbally or non-verbally?
- How do you believe they remember you?
- How would you like to be remembered by them?
- What did you do to make their life better?
- What did you do that might not have made their life better?

## Journey Around the World and the Impact of Teachers

### Background

My mother had 8 children with me being the youngest. Unfortunately, most of my brothers and sisters did not survive. Some of them passed away long before my memory fully developed and others before my birth. My mother explains to me that I was born in April of 1990, forty days before the holy month of Ramadan in the Islamic calendar. At the time, the government of Somalia was in its early demise before the ensuing chaos that took the lives of thousands of civilians and led to the displacement of many. It was a time of desperation, some families made it to neighboring countries in hopes of peace and prospects of prosperous futures (e.g., Ethiopia, Kenya, Djibouti etc.). Others were fortunate enough to be sponsored, emigrate and dwell in developed countries like the United States, United Kingdom and Canada. Many families remained in the region and migrated to other parts of the country that were less impacted by the government collapse. The Somali government collapse significantly impacted families that resided in and around the capital city of Mogadishu in the early stages of the civil war and later the civil war expanded to everywhere in the country.

As far as my family goes, my mother reports that she recalls we headed to a region that was not as impacted by the government collapse to buy some time and figure out where to go. My mother had all her children (6 of us, 4 boys and 2 girls not including the ones that had passed before my birth) with her and my father was separated from us by the war. It was a time of struggle, trauma and hardship for my family because as my mother says, "we did not know what was going to happen to us" or where exactly to go. After moving around for quite some time from city to city and town to town, my family returned to Mogadishu right before the United States entered the country to provide humanitarian aid and stability. The return to Mogadishu was encouraging for us because my uncle was a member of the United States military. My mother was hopeful that her brother was perhaps going to find us a way out of the country to somewhere safer. My uncle was able to secure us a flight from Mogadishu to neighboring country Kenya. We spent a night in Nairobi the capital city of Kenya, before heading to a refugee camp in Mombasa on the western part of the country along the coast.

## Mombasa

The refugee camp was in a remote town on the outskirts of Mombasa. It was a dumping place for many families displaced by the civil unrest later turned war and I say dumping place for a purposeful reason (explanation to come). Many of the families placed in the camp were hoping to go through a process (if all goes well) that would materialize in successful placement in the United States (UK or Canada) and the beginning of a new life away from the horrors that had stricken Somalia.

The refugee camp was located in a place similar to western Washington in terms of climate and weather pattern with warmer temperatures for mosquitos to lay their eggs and multiply in numbers. Consequently, many families lost their loved ones to a treatable disease like malaria. Going back to my calling of the refugee camp a dumping place- in this exact refugee camp is where two of my siblings passed away due to malaria. Prior to arriving at the refugee camp, my mother thought we (my family) and others were going to live in peace and harmony away from the chaos in Mogadishu. However, the opposite of her thoughts/hopes occurred- it was a nightmare and a horrific experience. It was as if the people organizing the camp miscalculated the threat mosquitos posed to the lives of those people to reside there prior to placement.

### From Mombasa to another refugee camp

At this point in time, my memory is starting to develop and I am beginning to soak in experiences and knowledge from my surroundings. That is, flashes of memory are beginning to unfold and solidify for me to be able to tell some parts of this story on my account as opposed to information gathered from others. Most of what I shared previously is information I gathered from interviewing multiple relatives and connecting those with my memories and the stories shared by my mother.

Back to the story- some time passes (not sure exactly how much) and the humanitarian aid organization decides to resettle the camp population from Mombasa to another camp in northeastern Kenya. The positive side of resettling the camp population to the new place appeared to be the organization admitting to their miscalculation of placing the camp population in Mombasa originally. The new camp as I remember was much warmer and drier than Mombasa. In addition, the humanitarian aid organization this time around provided the camp population with education about malaria and mosquito nets to protect themselves from mosquito bites. All in all, it was a much warmer place with somewhat less mosquitos.

After living there for a short period of time, our family decided to move to Nairobi (the capital city of Kenya) in hopes of securing better opportunities and the belief that our family had a better chance of relocating to the United States based on what others had shared. The drive from the refugee camp to Nairobi took one full day due to unpaved roads plus our location being near the border of Somalia and Nairobi's location being located in a more central part of the country.

### Nairobi

Living in Nairobi was a blessing in disguise to the development of my life and overall growth. I did not have anything in mind or what to expect prior to my family moving to

Nairobi. We came to find out Nairobi was much more developed and had better education system in comparison to the refugee camps we lived in previous years. Within the period of time my family lived in Nairobi, I witnessed the dispersion of my family to other parts and regions of the world. Some of my uncles found opportunities to resettle in the United States and United Kingdom while others returned home to Mogadishu. My mother had a decision to make since everyone in our family either found opportunities to resettle in the United States/United Kingdom, or had moved back to Somalia.

Within the short amount of time my mother had at the time, she decided to go back to Somalia and left my sister to live with her aunt in Nairobi. So, we headed back towards Somalia. I was apprehensive returning to Somalia because of the news that was developing from there in our years living in Kenya. My mother was aware of the instability in Somalia with regards to security, yet she had no other option. In our drive to back to Somalia, we stopped by my mother's sister to perhaps receive some funds that would enable us to continue the journey all the way to Mogadishu. We spent few months there and later continued with our journey to Somalia. Our journey came to a halt on the northeastern border of Somalia and Kenya due to insufficient funds. Fortunately, there were relatives there that took us in and as a result we spent more time there than we originally anticipated. At this point in time, I am nearing perhaps the age of pre-school or the age of beginning kindergarten.

This delay in our journey back to Mogadishu gave my mother time to rethink her decision to head back to Somalia. It was clear to my mother the future of us living in Somalia particularly Mogadishu was uncertain. Therefore, my mother decided to head back to Nairobi in pursuit of a life without fearing for our lives. Also, my mother knew the uncertainty of going back to Nairobi, a place we left not long ago. That is, we did not know with whom or where to stay. Like our journey to Mogadishu, we stopped by my aunt to help us return to Nairobi and obtain the proper documents to pass through border customs. As a result, we spent a significant amount of time there gathering the necessary paper work to successfully return to Nairobi. Months pass, our time to return to Nairobi comes and we successfully pass through border customs without encountering any issues due to my aunt's relationship with the local members of the government and her popularity in the community. We officially returned to Nairobi in mid-1997 on a hot sunny day full of uncertainty, yet with hope and optimism. I am aging closer to beginning formal education; however, my mother is in the process of securing a place for us to stay until she finds a stable home. In other words, beginning schooling is an afterthought at this point of my life.

A few hours later after our arrival in Nairobi, my mother encounters old neighbors from our days back in Mombasa (refugee camp). After exchanging greetings with them and my mother notifying them of our situation, they accepted to let us live with them. My mother was very happy about this development and early on took responsibility of preparing family meals, completing chores, buying groceries and taking charge of family budgeting. After we settled in our new home and new family, my mother enrolled me in a religious school. Enrollment in Muslim schools was expected as every child in the neighborhood attended such schools. They were also affordable and less complex in terms of registration and enrollment compared to non-religious public schools. As such, I began my formal education without any basic reading, and writing skills. In fact, I needed occupational therapy to help me fine tune my writing skills which was a foreign concept. Because of my low academic skills in reading and writing, the classroom teacher started me out with learning the Arabic alphabet and supported me with learning how to write using his own methods. He spent lots of one-on-one time to get me grounded on basic writing skills. The writing involved also reading the alphabet letters aloud whilst writing them to develop and accelerate my reading skills. In other words, he combined Arabic letter identification (ABC's of Arabic) with letter sounds (phonics). After a few months of receiving this intervention, I graduated to learning how to read words and later sentences. I highly benefited from the support given by the classroom teacher as he knew I was determined to learn. My progression was primarily due to my eagerness to learn and inner motivation to achieve mastery.

## Beginning non-religious public school

I always wanted to go to school like the kids in my neighborhood. Most kids attending the religious school I attended also attended non-religious public schools which increased my desire to want to attend even more so. In addition, I thought school was fun based on what other kids in my neighborhood shared. Consequently, all that students in my religious school talked about was school this, school that. I felt school was the next place for me to be and thought it would be fun. The idea of attending non-religious public school did not cross my mother's mind nor did I bug her about it. Although I was a kid, I was aware of my surroundings and the financial support required to enroll me in school.

The idea of me attending public school was planted in my mother's mind by a distant aunt. She also convinced and encouraged mother to enroll me in public school stating my future heavily depended on it. Consequently, my mother enrolled me in public school with money she borrowed from others. Because my mother was not able to pay my school fees in full, it meant that almost every week I was sent home to bring the money. And every week my mother told me to tell the school finance department that she promises to get the money next week. She sure did not have the full amount of money required; however, she was hopeful and did not want me to miss significant instruction time and learning.

Starting 1st grade had its ups and downs. Like religious school, I was required to read and write at the level of some other first graders who had pre-school and kindergarten experience, but in English and Swahili, not Arabic. I did not know how to read and write in these languages. The classroom teacher did not have time to teach me the basic academic skills any more than other kids in her class. I felt like I was drowning and helpless. However, I knew I could teach myself how to read and write. I began with learning how to write letters although it took me significant time.

### The first standardized academic assessment comes

This was by far the most difficult educational experience to date yet the most positive and uplifting. In the first standardized testing, students were required to read long passages in English and Swahili. What made this a hard experience was that the teacher and I both knew I had no clue how to read both passages. I felt hurt and angry, but I knew I could learn how to read. So I began the process of learning how to read Swahili and English. I began with letter identification and asked students with far better reading skills to tell me the letter sounds associated with each letter in the alphabet. I annoyed a couple of students asking them the same questions while providing them with humor and a reason to feel better about themselves. To get an idea of how much learning/progress took place in my reading, the next standardized academic assessment was the measuring tool to answer that very question.

Standardized assessments were administered after every 2 months. The examination date arrives, and I start to read the passages with a bit of anxiety and excitement to see how much progress I have made. Somehow, I was able to correctly read the English passage without any difficulties; however, I made multiple errors reading the Swahili passages. The problem here was that the rules of reading are different in these languages. In fact, reading Swahili is far less complicated than English yet I struggled a bit with Swahili because of errors switching from English to Swahili.

From there onwards, I kept focusing on areas I needed to improve and similarly made progress in each area of academic weakness. I began to experience success in school and became known as an avid student. In other words, I was considered a "genius" based on my successes in standardizing testing. My name was mentioned around the school after the completion of every standardized test. Students were ranked based on their performances in all areas of academic testing and were recognized for their performance- I was a usual participant in those recognition ceremonies for my performance.

At this point in time, my mother found an opportunity to immigrate to the United States with other relatives. This also meant that my mother had to immigrate to the United States without me. It was a difficult decision for my mother to make; however, it was one she made with my future in mind. My mother immigrated to the United States and it resulted in a better financial state for my sister and me. It also meant that I would begin living with my sister. It was a difficult transition period for me mainly due to the impact my mother had on my overall development. My sister was able to secure after-school tutoring provided by my second-grade teacher to supplement my overall academic development. The tutoring allowed me to improve my academic development in reading and writing.

After few years of living with my sister, she also was able to secure an opportunity to immigrate to the United States without me. This also meant I had to start all over and start living with my closest aunt whom my sister lived with for many years. It also impacted my psychological development, it made me feel all alone; however, my teacher providing tutoring services, encouraged me to stay the course and continue to pursue higher education. She played a big role in keeping me grounded and helped me focus on my schooling. She also played a big role in my emotional development by ensuring that I did not feel alone and that someday I will be reunited with my mother and sister. She instilled hope in me and a reason to keep going.

## Life in Minneapolis

Time works in mysterious ways. I never imagined life in the United States let alone reunification with mother and sister. However, the latter occurred, and I was very happy to see my mother again.

I did not know how to embrace my mother. I cried and cried, it was all tears of joy and gratitude to all the prayers I made as a kid when mother left for the United States.

Life in Minneapolis came with its challenges of acculturation, the starting of a new life, new school, new friends and reestablishment. Fortunately, I had a strong academic background, and this was evident when I was first examined by a school personnel to get a baseline of my academic standing. This process was eased by uncle's unwavering support and understanding. He also was a firm believer in my ability to achieve great things academically. Educators in my new school also were surprised to learn of my advanced reading and writing skills. I was quickly mainstreamed in most of my classes in the general education classrooms with the few exceptions. My reading and math skills were more advanced than my peers; however, my writing skills needed some improvement. The educators in my new school supported me unconditionally but they did not challenge me like my teacher in Nairobi.

## Kent

After a few years of living in Minneapolis, my sister requested that I live with her in Kent Washington. She believed Kent offered better educational system than Minneapolis. Also, I wanted to live in Washington mainly because of its attractive climate. I found the harsh winters in Minneapolis hard to get accustomed to. Kent Washington was the place that truly challenged me to achieve more in terms of academic development.

I began my schooling in Kentridge High School, a place to this day I owe some of my educational success. I consider Kentridge High School the birth of my educational growth. The educators there provided me with exceptional instruction and instilled confidence in all the students in the ELL program. Within a semester I graduated to taking classes with regular education students propelled by my success in the ELL program. The teachers in the ELL program felt that I would succeed in any given program based on my determination and work ethic. I was always motivated to learn and master anything I set my eyes on. It has always been the support of educators who saw a promise in me and educators who guided me when I needed guidance as well as assistance to carry on. I found all that in Kent, Washington. I graduated from Kentridge High School with unlimited support from my teachers.

Even with the success achieved, there were barriers along the way in the form of educators' shortcomings and limited knowledge. Some educators associated ELL students with lack of academic knowledge and left them unchallenged. This pattern of educators not challenging ELL students continued until I began my junior year in high school. My 11th grade English teacher was one of the best teachers at that time. She challenged me to write more, to read more and to achieve more in terms of education. As a result of her unwavering support and countless hours of mentoring, teaching, and guidance, I was able to improve my writing. Whereas others early on in my education lowered academic expectations, she raised expectations and challenged me to improve in every academic area. By the time I was in 12th grade, my writing was much more advanced purely due to her support and teaching. I was also on track to graduate and had achieved all the graduation requirements including passing state examinations in my first year of testing.

## College

I honestly did not know if I was going to attend college despite having the aspirations to do so. I had difficulties navigating through the financial aid system. I was the first in my family to have the aspiration to attend college which meant nobody in my family had prior knowledge of the process involved.

In my final year of high school, I received tremendous support from my counselor to apply for financial aid and colleges to attend. I received acceptance to many of the colleges I applied to; however, they required me to take loans to cover my tuition and living expenses. I did not feel comfortable taking loans for many reasons and opted to not do so. Consequently, I returned to Kentridge High School in the summer before my freshmen year of college to notify my counselor of the circumstance. Long story short, I was able to attend college with the kindness of an educator who knew the power of education and who saw a promise in me.

In summary, I am now at the final stages of achieving my master's degree. That is, soon I am hoping to finish my schooling and become a school psychologist. This process began 2 and half years ago with many obstacles along the way. I was fortunate to have some educators who believed in me throughout this process of educational development. In fact, I had educators who believed in me since the beginning of my educational career. Some educators also led to barriers in my development in many forms and shapes. The simplest barriers educators had emanated from their belief systems. Many educators in the past did challenge me while others did the opposite. Other educators simply instilled confidence and belief in me. The barriers primarily emanated from educators limited knowledge and understanding. I always wanted to be given the opportunity to learn and grow with unwavering support, understanding, patience, validity and acceptance. I just wanted to be treated fairly while being given the time and patience to learn. The determination, perseverance, resilience and motivation were all within me; however, I needed educators to allow me to learn with care, kindness, and unconditional positive regard.

**Reflection:**

Now that you have read the story and thought about the questions, it is time to reflect.

- What did you think about when you read this story?
- How can that help you in dealing with current and future students?
- How can that help you in dealing with current and future parents?
- How can that help you in dealing with current and future colleagues?
- What can you do differently starting today, to achieve better results (even if you started with good results)?

# Manipulation or Being Manipulated

This story examines the concept of how we attribute meaning to words and actions that may or may not actually be appropriate or correct. And, sometimes we don't even know we are doing it.

### Things to think about when reading this story:

- As you read this story, can you relate to it personally?
- Have you ever worked with a student, colleague or parent who was similar?
- What messages did you send to that student, colleague, or parent verbally or non-verbally?
- How do you believe they remember you?
- How would you like to be remembered by them?
- What did you do to make their life better?
- What did you do that might not have made their life better?

## Manipulation or Being Manipulated

We create additional meanings for many of our words, and often it is through connotations, negative or positive. If we use the word manipulation when we are talking about children, we usually put a negative connotation on the word.

As humans, we are manipulating our environment from a very early age. When a baby cries, they are usually crying due to pain, be that hunger pains, an uncomfortable (and full) diaper, or some other pain. They will manipulate the adults in their environment to go through a series of steps. First, check that diaper. If it is clean, then try feeding the baby. If that doesn't work, it is usually a panic call to "mom."

Do we think about babies manipulating us? Do we see this as negative? Usually we don't think about it as manipulation and we don't see it as negative.

We grow up learning certain behaviors to get what we want, even if we don't know that we are doing those behaviors…

The other day I was working with a teacher. She had written feedback during a re-evaluation of a student for special education, "He argues about things that just are not important!" When I went to talk with her, we ended up talking for quite some time. She was clearly rather frustrated with the behavior of this 1st grade student, and she strongly believed he was being manipulative. I challenged that belief and talked about whether or not it really is manipulation. After the meeting, I realized that what I had said was not worded quite correctly. I was fighting against the negative connotations that go with the word manipulation, instead of fighting against whether or not it was manipulation.

Later that afternoon I spoke with someone who knows the family very well and got insight into the family. This little boy relies heavily on his mother, and has learned that certain behaviors on his part get him what he wants. The puzzle pieces from the discussion that occurred earlier, with the teacher, started to fall into place. The teacher mentioned that he appears to argue just to argue, even when he is clearly wrong. If he gets something wrong during math (we are talking addition and subtraction, not multi-variable calculus here), he will argue with her that he is right and she is wrong, even when she shows him the answer using "manipulatives." Funny how that word showed up again….

This child has learned that he can have his way at times by arguing. He hates being wrong (lots of folks do), and he has learned to argue until the other person (usually his mother) just gives in to him. And he has carried this behavior into his interactions with others, like with his teacher.

Now, is he actually being manipulative? Is he manipulating the teacher? What connotation are we placing on this word this time? Are we putting energy into something that does not actually matter? That is, wouldn't we be better off putting our efforts into teaching new behaviors than spending time on putting negativity toward something that could be a natural behavioral development for some children?

This is a little boy who is demonstrating a behavior that is not appropriate. It is not the behavior in and of itself that is inappropriate, the behavior is inappropriate because it is harmful to him as a learner. If we get stuck on looking at this behavior related to him being "manipulative," we will be stuck without any idea of how we might be able to modify the behavior over time. He is doing this behavior because it works for him. Our job is to look into how we can teach him to accept that he cannot always have his way and how he can get his wants and needs met in a more appropriate manner.

As babies, we cry until someone else feeds us. Then, those same people teach us how to prepare our own food. Then, sometime in the future we feed babies because they cry, and we eventually teach them how to feed themselves. Manipulation is not always a negative, but is always a behavior that is speaking to others, communicating wants, needs and is a sign of a lack of socially appropriate problem solving at a certain age.

As educators, we need to first think about what skills we can teach and make sure we are not supporting, or reinforcing, negative behaviors. Therefore, look at manipulative behaviors as an indicator regarding the skills we need to teach.

Ross Greene has written excellent books that center around, "they would if they could…." This is all about children wanting to be successful, and most of the poor behaviors are a lack of appropriate skills necessary to get their needs met. These books are well worth the time if this area interests you.

**Reflection:**

Now that you have read the story and thought about the questions, it is time to reflect.

- What did you think about when you read this story?
- How can that help you in dealing with current and future students?
- How can that help you in dealing with current and future parents?
- How can that help you in dealing with current and future colleagues?
- What can you do differently starting today, to achieve better results (even if you started with good results)?

# Invisible Disabilities

Our eyes play tricks on us at times or can mislead us. We might not treat people fairly due to how we have perceived a situation or a person. Invisible disabilities, like learning disabilities, can and do create problems for people that can and do last a lifetime.

There are two other similar stories in this book, one on living with a disability and one on what is a disability, from the perspective of someone who has a disability. In case you are skipping around and missed them.

**Things to think about when reading this story:**

- As you read this story, can you relate to it personally?
- Have you ever worked with a student, colleague or parent who was similar?
- What messages did you send to that student, colleague, or parent verbally or non-verbally?
- How do you believe they remember you?
- How would you like to be remembered by them?
- What did you do to make their life better?
- What did you do that might not have made their life better?

## Invisible Disabilities

I asked some people this morning whether or not it would make any sense to share my personal story, and they encouraged me to do so.

As a child, I had such extreme articulation issues that I was unintelligible to all but close family members. Also, I struggled (even more) with Aphasia (sometimes words that I know, sometimes people's names that I know just will not come out, even if I can see the word in my mind as a picture). This was so extreme that my parent's friends convinced them that I must have been "retarded," using the term of the time. I know some folks can find some humor in that, not the least of which is wondering whether or not we ever figured that one out…. ☺

After a staff meeting a couple of people commented on my abilities as a public speaker (in a positive way). This also happens when I speak in other districts or at conferences. However, that is not my personal experience when I am speaking.

What I hear is every mistake I make in pronouncing words. I also hear and feel every time I cannot make a word come out, a word I know, and I need to create a whole new sentence to get across what I had hoped to say. Over the years I have gotten past the frustration, but it is still not fun.

I am telling you about this, because, like you, as a school psychologist I see and work with many students who have disabilities that are not visible. If we see a student who needs a wheelchair, we understand (at some levels) why they cannot walk. There is nothing visible about learning disabilities or speech/language disabilities. We as educators are doing everything we can to help all children learn, yet sometimes we can become frustrated when we teach something and it is not learned. Our frustration, though, does not begin to match the frustration many of our students feel and experience, and believe me, that frustration can go on for a lifetime.

My hope for writing this is to put out there a message for hope that, with enough kindness, caring, and work, kids can find ways to work around their disabilities and that when we are feeling frustrated we need to dig deep into our reserves, given that our students are likely more frustrated than we are (even if it doesn't look that way at times).

**Reflections:**

Now that you have read the story and thought about the questions, it is time to reflect.

- What did you think about when you read this story?
- How can that help you in dealing with current and future students?
- How can that help you in dealing with current and future parents?
- How can that help you in dealing with current and future colleagues?
- What can you do differently starting today, to achieve better results (even if you started with good results)?

# Facing Challenges and Believing in Yourself

This story examines a veteran teacher taking on a very challenging child. learning each day from this opportunity, and how we need to believe in ourselves in order to achieve the results we want, and need to achieve for our students.

**Things to think about when reading this story:**

- As you read this story, can you relate to it personally?
- Have you ever worked with a student, colleague or parent who was similar?
- What messages did you send to that student, colleague, or parent verbally or non-verbally?
- How do you believe they remember you?
- How would you like to be remembered by them?
- What did you do to make their life better?
- What did you do that might not have made their life better?

## Facing Challenges and Believing in Yourself

This is my twenty fifth and last year of teaching. I began teaching in 1978 and then stayed home to raise our daughters from 1987 to 2000. This year's class, with 26 students, is the largest number of students I've had since the mid-eighties.

Our self-contained teacher, Jill, first approached me in August, before school started, to tell me she wanted to integrate two first grade students into my class. In the past, this meant joining my general education class for lunch, PE, music and any special projects we thought the child could handle. She then specifically mentioned Suzy and said she thought she should be in my class for most of the day as she needed the general education student models and, though below standard, some of the academics. I immediately thought to myself, not this year, the class is already big enough, and just nodded each time she approached me and essentially put her off with a smile. Suzy is a darling little girl who is significantly impacted by her autism. Suzy struggles with communicating her needs and with social skills, and this often leads to meltdowns that are intense. I could not envision how Suzy could be in my classroom all day long, and I didn't know how I would deal with Suzy when she was having a significant problem.

When Suzy joined us for lunch each day I could see that she had come a long way behaviorally since kindergarten when I heard her crying many times during a school day. Suzy could open her own lunch and although "a picky eater" she eats and cleans up without assistance. She became more and more comfortable and one day in October put her lunch box in our coat closet and announced that she was going back to room 4 (the Support Center) to get her backpack. She did and hung it in our closet. Suzy had moved in.

I had a conversation with Jill and said, "What's one more. Let's try it!" So, Suzy made the transition to my first-grade classroom without a one-on-one support person. Although I have had some interaction with children with Autism, this has proven to be a great learning experience and eye opener for me. Working with Suzy has deepened my understanding of the significant amount of patience and nurturing needed to work with children with Autism. The calmer I am, the more successful Suzy and I are at finding solutions to problems we are having. It is about us working together, even if she is not fully aware of what our efforts mean. I have also noticed that the other students watch me carefully, so positive reactions from me are important for all of us. I have also learned not to fight every battle. For Suzy, making her comfortable enough to learn in the general education classroom may just be my acceptance of who she is in the moment. That is, she is clearly learning very important social and behavioral skills by watching and imitating her peers, something that is difficult to achieve in a self-contained special education classroom.

Looking back, maybe we should have slowly transitioned her to part of the day, but since Suzy initiated the move, we dove right in. To be honest, it has taken a great deal of love and patience. I think a teacher with less experience in the classroom would have to fight hard not to doubt his or her abilities. After this many years of teaching I have a fairly big bag of tricks, but am having to come up with new ones to make sure Suzy's social and emotional needs are being met without either of us getting too frustrated. Her emotions are unpredictable and it is a lesson in perseverance to understand what she needs and how to help her calm herself. Luckily Jill is available to help with breathing techniques, fidget toys and a hug. Sometimes it's as simple as calling Mom to bring the pajamas that were forgotten for pajama day or singing a song to distract her.

Other times the meltdowns are loud and intense and I must figure out what to do. This is when self-confidence in one's teaching skills is critical to success. I have learned that Suzy, although she has trouble communicating, will often give me the clues I need if I just remain calm and listen. Unlike a support center classroom there is only one adult in mine…me! and my 25 other students have had to be patient and self-sufficient while I tend to Suzy.

Suzy has developed enough trust in me, that when I stay calm and listen, she helps me understand her needs or wants. For example, one day when she was not able to tell me what she wanted (and she was trying very hard), she took me to another student who had what she wanted and showed it to me, saying, "he has." Another day, Suzy wanted a glue stick, and I gave her one. She repeatedly told me, "no, new one." I was giving her a new one, so I was confused. Then, I realized that she did not believe it was new because it was on my desk (and that I had not taken it out of the cupboard). I learned that trying to reason through something like this is not a good use of time, and instead I am very careful regarding any "battle" I choose to take on. This letting go has helped me become a better guide in the classroom.

The work on trust building has been crucial for Suzy and me. It has become very clear over time that our ability to work together has grown as her trust in me has grown. She understands that I am going to work very hard to help her meet her wants and needs. This has also allowed me a greater ability to tell her "no" when she is doing something inappropriate and have a much higher likelihood that she will respond in a neutral or positive manner. This is important, given that sometimes what she wants is not appropriate at that time.

To meet Suzy's academic goals/needs (like reading) we are going to either send her to the support center several times a day or use a push in model to work in a small group in my room. We know that she is learning a great deal in our general education classroom, but we also know that she needs additional direct instruction to make sure she has learned a new concept. Our school psychologist, Jeff, helps me with ideas and encouragement. We are staying open and flexible. It isn't easy but I am up for the challenge and I want to do what is best for Suzy.

Teachers with fewer years of experience might find inclusion of a child like Suzy daunting, but if you desire to learn and grow as a teacher, you too will find a way to make a positive difference. This experience will also help you learn about student behavior in general, and make your "bag of tools/tricks" more powerful and larger than most any other experience could or would. Believe in your skills as a professional. Inclusion is difficult but rewarding, tiring but energizing, frustrating and worth it!

**Reflection:**

Now that you have read the story and thought about the questions, it is time to reflect.

- What did you think about when you read this story?
- How can that help you in dealing with current and future students?
- How can that help you in dealing with current and future parents?
- How can that help you in dealing with current and future colleagues?
- What can you do differently starting today, to achieve better results (even if you started with good results)?

# It is results, not beliefs

Whether it is doctors referring patients to their friends, because they like them or if it is educators believing in others because they like them, neither is likely to lead to great results. Often people confuse liking something or someone with something being "good" or "useful." We are in the role of helping children. We need to examine whether or not we are helping our children to learn and achieve, and we need to base this upon data, not hopes nor dreams.

By the way, it is highly likely that we could achieve this without testing our kids as much as we are testing them, most other nations (the ones outperforming us) do.

**Things to think about when reading this story:**

- As you read this story, can you relate to it personally?
- Have you ever worked with a student, colleague or parent who was similar?
- What messages did you send to that student, colleague, or parent verbally or non-verbally?
- How do you believe they remember you?
- How would you like to be remembered by them?
- What did you do to make their life better?
- What did you do that might not have made their life better?

## It is results, not beliefs

Within education, it is somewhat rare for a school district to know their own data in any area outside reading, math, or discipline. And, these areas tend to only be known in direct relationship to what is likely to end up in a local newspaper.

I have spent a large portion of my career trying to work on disproportionality issues, and I have seen changes at the local level for many districts. The changes tend to occur after educators within the district have seen their own data, and have seen how poorly some aspect of their system is working. Educators are good and caring people, and the poor results are rarely known outside the areas of reading, math and discipline.

There has been disproportionality in the areas of ELL/Special Education, Gifted/Talented Education, AP classes, discipline and other areas that has existed since we started paying attention in the late 1960s. However, on the larger systems level of our country as a whole, this has not changed.

Within education, we are known to change much slower than other major areas, like science or medicine. Dan Lortie was one of the first researchers to write about this, and his belief was that we change slowly because most of us have never left education and it has worked for us. That is, most of us went from elementary, to middle school, to high school, to college to teaching or working in the schools. Also, most of us found success within the system. Therefore, why would we want to change anything?

With education being a very slow system to change and with many of our problems being unknown to us, we need to look at some of the "why's" to this problem. It has already been noted that we don't have our data in many of the areas around disproportionality. If we hear about problems in this area, we are likely to think that it is "the other guy" if we do not have our own data. Also, like each profession, we protect our own. The other staff members are often our friends and we often believe that they are doing a good job, because we like them. However, these beliefs are based on something that is not likely to be related to student success. They are based on how much we like one another and believe in one another. However, belief and liking do not equal success.

I was doing a training in the southern portion of Washington State, and someone came to me during a break to talk about the great work they had done in their previous district. I asked them how they knew it was great work, and they talked about the wonderful people they were working with, how smart everyone was, and how accomplished everyone was…. I again asked how they knew that the work had been great work, and they started to repeat what they had already told me. Then, I asked whether or not they had any proof, any data, to support that the work was great work. They answered, "no." I repeated my question regarding how they knew it was great work, and they returned to discussing how great everyone on the team was, and how accomplished they were…. In the end, they did not have any evidence that the work they had done had a positive impact on the children or any impact at all, positive, negative, or neutral.

As we do our work, we need to be very careful to not fall into the trap of thinking it is great work simply because we did the work, or we really liked and respected those we were working with during the project.

Also, if we controlled all or most of the variables in our research, we cannot believe it is great work. Great work is work in which we can measure a positive impact on our children. This is about how our kids are doing based upon how well our system taught them and not on some research study that controlled all the variables. How well did we help them grow in a way that will improve their post school outcomes?

**Reflection:**

Now that you have read the story and thought about the questions, it is time to reflect.

- What did you think about when you read this story?
- How can that help you in dealing with current and future students?
- How can that help you in dealing with current and future parents?
- How can that help you in dealing with current and future colleagues?
- What can you do differently starting today, to achieve better results (even if you started with good results)?

# Can, Can't, or Didn't…

The simple fact that a student didn't do something for us does not mean they cannot do the task. Or, maybe they "cannot" do it today, but through working with them, they will be able to do it sooner than later.

Also, parents respond better to hearing their child "didn't demonstrate" versus "can't do it."

**Things to think about when reading this story:**

- As you read this story, can you relate to it personally?
- Have you ever worked with a student, colleague or parent who was similar?
- What messages did you send to that student, colleague, or parent verbally or non-verbally?
- How do you believe they remember you?
- How would you like to be remembered by them?
- What did you do to make their life better?
- What did you do that might not have made their life better?

## Can, Can't, or Didn't

Over the years I have seen many situations between schools and parents devolve into misery over arguments about what a student can and "cannot" do. This is usually, but not always, the school telling the parent, "little Johnny can't _____." Then, the parents respond, "I don't know what you are talking about, because he can do it at home."

There are times in which the parents are telling the truth, there are times in which the parents are in denial regarding the disability of their child (and really believe that their child can do something they cannot yet do), and there are times in which the parent is deflecting (it might be easier to argue about a trivial issue than discuss some hard truths). In the end, though, all of these arguments lead to the same end: nowhere valuable for the child.

There are more possibilities than noted above, but what does it really matter? Would you rather be right, or would you rather help the child?

Last year (and this year), and I guess years before that, our school has struggled with a specific parent who believes her child possesses skills far beyond those ever demonstrated in the school setting. However, this year was the first year in which the parent has left an IEP meeting with a smile on her face and visited with the staff. The norm before that had been arguments and hard feelings.

Instead of spending time subtly trying to argue or prove her wrong, we agreed to work out a new approach that would follow some of her suggestions and try to get this child to demonstrate his skills within the school setting. With this new approach, the parent eagerly agreed to help us reinforce our efforts with her son. She believes that he just is not doing something because he doesn't believe that we will hold him accountable. The interesting part of this is that this has allowed us to have other conversations with her that are as important or even more important. For example, if a student is not demonstrating a skill across multiple environments and independently, then the skill is of limited value, possibly of very little value.

Therefore, "can," "cannot" and "doesn't" really come to the front of the discussion. Instead of wasting time on "cannot," we need to focus on "didn't" and "doesn't." This allows the parents and school staff to have deep discussions about the "why." Why isn't Johnny demonstrating the important skill within the school environment? Do we need to teach the skill or change something within the environment in order for the skill to be usable? Is the skill we are concerned about the correct skill? For example, if we are trying to teach long-division (such an important life skill), and the student does not have their multiplication reasonably mastered, are we using our time and effort in the best way? Or, if we are trying to teach a child to ask for help instead of having a meltdown, do they know how to ask for help? Do they know when to ask for help (before things are too serious)? Do they know how to tell when things are getting too serious? And, do they trust us to help them?

There are many educational and behavioral experts that agree that kids want to be successful and that they will do the right thing if they can. Therefore, most of the time we need to look at problems through the lens of "doesn't." This lens will help us to focus on whether or not the student has the prerequisite skills to have a good chance of "can do it." Also, focusing skills takes us away from the dangerous ground of "bad kid" or "unmotivated kid," both of which almost always lead us to failure, for the kids and for us.

Last, when we focus on teaching skills and believing that students are just not doing something because they don't know how (versus cannot), this helps us build relationships with both the parents and the students. The parents see us as trying to better understand their child and help their child and the children see us as believing in them as capable of learning any new skill.

**Reflection:**

Now that you have read the story and thought about the questions, it is time to reflect.

- What did you think about when you read this story?
- How can that help you in dealing with current and future students?
- How can that help you in dealing with current and future parents?
- How can that help you in dealing with current and future colleagues?
- What can you do differently starting today, to achieve better results (even if you started with good results)?

# How do you see yourself...?

This story focuses in on whether or not our self-doubts are being transferred to our children and/or our students. Are we aware of the messages we are sending to our children through our choices of wording?

**Things to think about when reading this story:**

- As you read this story, can you relate to it personally?
- Have you ever worked with a student, colleague or parent who was similar?
- What messages did you send to that student, colleague, or parent verbally or non-verbally?
- How do you believe they remember you?
- How would you like to be remembered by them?
- What did you do to make their life better?
- What did you do that might not have made their life better?

### How do you see yourself? How do our kids see themselves? And can our doubts hinder our kids?

Here I am in the process of writing this book with my wife and co-author, and all of the great people who are contributing to this process, and something really hit me…

Many of my colleagues who agreed to contribute their stories are struggling to do so. What I am hearing is: I am not a writer, I cannot write. Sometimes I hear nothing at all from some people with wonderful stories to tell.

One of the contributors with an amazing story took months to write it (a little more than 2 pages) and had many, many friends read it in the process. Another person who contributed a great story told me, "I am not a writer, you will help me, right?" Yet another person said, "I cannot do it!" I interviewed this person and she told me several amazing stories. I then put them into writing for her and she edited them. I know she could have written them herself.

As a young man, going through school, then off to college and on to graduate school, I was a very weak writer. Given that my ideas were decent and I did well on tests, most people just ignored the fact that I was a poor writer and I literally never had anyone, until I was completing my internship, address this issue. My intern supervisor (25+ years later still a good friend and mentor to me), after reading my first evaluation report, told me, "This is terrible, how did you make it through school?" That would have been devastating, if it were not for the fact that he took it upon himself to teach me how to write decent reports. That was a mountain of work for him and for me, and a huge supply of red ink pens!!!

As the years progressed, I have learned to be a decent writer and have now written 6 books. Yet, I struggled to see myself as a writer until about the third or fourth book.

Is it possible that our own self-doubts could be transferred on to our students??? I believe that anyone who graduated from college, such as teachers, principals, and school psychologists, are writers. Think about the number of essays you had to write to make it through college. Of course, there are a lot of folks who never went to college who are also writers. I am just saying, it is hard to validate the concept of "I am not a writer" for someone who made it through college. These folks might be saying they don't like to write or are expressing self-doubts, but they are writers. Then, from that point, getting really good at it is a matter of desire and practice.

Back to our kids. If we don't see ourselves as writers, a skill that is critically important for our students (especially in the age of Common Core), what are the subtle messages that we are sending our students? Also, are we even sending not so subtle messages, like, "I also struggle with writing…."

There is nothing wrong with telling students, "I also struggle with _____," if you go on to tell them how to get past the struggles.

Is it possible that we can tell our students how to get past a struggle if we have not worked our way through the same basic problem? We, of course, will not have solved all of the problems we could face in life. However, we are all capable writers. Therefore, we have solved this problem. As educators, it is also highly likely that we also have good skills in reading and math, but some students hear the "I am not good at math" message, also.

This story is about two things to me. First, are we really being fair with ourselves? And, second, what messages are we sending our students when we have our own internal struggles with confidence in a subject? There is nothing wrong with having struggles, we all do. However, if the struggle is not strongly based in a reality we might be rather unfair with ourselves. We might also pass on messages to our students that can impact their confidence, and their willingness to face certain challenges.

So, please take a few minutes to think about your self-confidence in these areas. Then, think about what messages, subtle or not, you send to students about the areas that are difficult for you.

In the end, it is great for our kids to know that we also struggle in some areas. However, it is even more important for them to learn how we have faced and overcome the hurdles in our life.

**Reflection:**

Now that you have read the story and thought about the questions, it is time to reflect.

- What did you think about when you read this story?
- How can that help you in dealing with current and future students?
- How can that help you in dealing with current and future parents?
- How can that help you in dealing with current and future colleagues?
- What can you do differently starting today, to achieve better results (even if you started with good results)?

# Helping a Child Change Their Internal Dialogue

This story focuses on the incredible growth a student can make if they see themselves having the potential to do well. Also, this talks about changing that internal dialogue, a necessary change to succeed.

**Things to think about when reading this story:**

- As you read this story, can you relate to it personally?
- Have you ever worked with a student, colleague or parent who was similar?
- What messages did you send to that student, colleague, or parent verbally or non-verbally?
- How do you believe they remember you?
- How would you like to be remembered by them?
- What did you do to make their life better?
- What did you do that might not have made their life better?

## Helping a Child Change Their Internal Dialogue

It was the year our district had made the decision to close our primary (K-3) School Adjustment programs and send some of the students back to their home schools (School Adjustment is the name that that district uses for its program that serves children with behavioral disabilities). This was a program for students with social, emotional, and/or behavioral needs. I basically provided the needed behavior intervention assistance district-wide, working with a variety of students pre-K to 21. This year presented a new challenge. This was the year that I spent almost 8 out of 9 months in one building basically as a 1:1 paraeducator with one of these 3$^{rd}$ grade students.

He was a child qualified for special education in the category of Emotional Behavioral Disability. I was told "with many maladjusted behaviors." The "honeymoon" lasted maybe 2 days before signs of why he had been placed into a special program became apparent. At the age of 9 he could cuss with the best of them and would often elope out of the building. When I was called out to observe him I was given the list of behaviors they were already seeing and was told he was literally "climbing the walls." While the exaggeration was not far off, as he could definitely climb as demonstrated by climbing the backstop of the baseball field, he didn't quite climb walls. When he would get upset it often included bad language, eloping, hitting, and sometimes throwing something. After my first observation, I knew this was going to be a challenging year!

To understand how we progressed with this student is to first understand the culture of this school. This was a fully functioning PBIS model school! The principal had developed and cultivated a culture unlike many of the schools I was often called to assist in. This particular school had all the right things going on, such as school wide expectations for every area of the school. The principal even taught some of the expectations (bathroom rules and expectation) the first week as the role model for all. All of the staff had buy in to the school wide system of "oops slips" and "super job" tickets and staff were encouraged and even recognized for using the "Super Jobs". This was a school that knew how to provide a positive learning environment and yet still hold students accountable with reasonable consequences.

However, this young man was a first for many staff and, quite honestly, their building. It's not every day a school suddenly needs to program for such a unique student. Once a month our team which included myself, the special education teacher, general education teacher, principal, counselor, psychologist, para(s), and sometimes others met to discuss this one particular student. Every month we reviewed the data on his behaviors and discussed if our interventions were helping to improve those behaviors or not. It was trial and error to begin with but as the year continued we found a formula that started to work. This was a process!! None of us had a blueprint for what to do or how to do it. We took best practices from different places and melded them together to create a plan that worked for this child.

I spent the first days/months filling his emotional "bucket" with something he had had very little of, unfortunately, and that was positive feedback. He had been told from previous teachers, paras, principals, his siblings and his parents that he was a "bad" kid. Half way through the year we found out his mom had their church perform an "exorcism" to rid the evils from him. These were messages that were not easy for us to "undo." This was a child that needed to know he was a good kid, that he was loved, and that he was capable of great things. How was I going to help do that? I spent the first few days finding every possible positive I could. He received points that generated into "Super Star" tickets. He received a ton of these tickets. I wanted to flip the script playing in this child's head. I wanted to help him flip the negative script and flip the choices he often made. I provided a "door out" often and we took many a lap around the building to cool off, talk, and understand where his frustrations came from. I validated his feelings and offered a non-judgmental ear to his concerns. There were also firm consequences. They were often quick and to the point. He rarely missed recess but would often owe me a minute here and there for cussing. It was the reset he needed to remind him he could change. He initially got many more "oops slips" before a firm consequence happened as well. He made more "oops" than his peers, but our goal was to teach him what to do different, not only to punish because he couldn't. I 100 percent believed that this was a child that WOULD if only he COULD.

Each month he improved, we increased our expectations and I slightly faded some of the more intense support. Each month he improved, his spirits and overall wellbeing improved. By May of that school year I was able to transfer what I was providing 1:1 to a para who would support him through his 4th grade year. I followed up with him each year after I moved on to other students in our district. After 2 years he no longer needed a 1:1 para. At his 6th grade re-evaluation, after 4 years of intervention, and 4 years at a school that never gave up, he no longer qualified for Special Education services as EBD (emotional/behavioral disability). What a celebration!! I was excited to throw him a pizza party at the end of his 6th grade year to celebrate the incredible successes he had achieved. I cheered him for all the hard work HE put in to make the changes necessary to not only be a great student but a great person. A person he could feel proud of, a person he could love, a person worthy of it all!! He was probably one of the most challenging students I worked with and yet through it all he was absolutely the most rewarding!!

**Reflection:**

Now that you have read the story and thought about the questions, it is time to reflect.

- What did you think about when you read this story?
- How can that help you in dealing with current and future students?
- How can that help you in dealing with current and future parents?
- How can that help you in dealing with current and future colleagues?
- What can you do differently starting today, to achieve better results (even if you started with good results)?

# They Just Are Not Motivated.... Really?

This story challenges the thoughts and beliefs that a child, any child, is just not motivated. Also, this challenges the reader to think about how a different approach can lead to success much more often for our children.

### Things to think about when reading this story:

- As you read this story, can you relate to it personally?
- Have you ever worked with a student, colleague or parent who was similar?
- What messages did you send to that student, colleague, or parent verbally or non-verbally?
- How do you believe they remember you?
- How would you like to be remembered by them?
- What did you do to make their life better?
- What did you do that might not have made their life better?

### They Just Are Not Motivated…. Really?

It was a really weird year. I was split between three schools and in the middle of every day I taught 2 periods in the behaviorally disabled students' classroom. I had done a lot of interventions, but I had never taught this type of class. I heard many times throughout my time there that "they" are just not motivated, referring to a lot of the students in this class.

Entering into this classroom, I wanted to use motivators that could make the situation easier and better for both the students and for me.

I created a big plan of different options for the students and had a way for them to earn all kinds of different things throughout the course of any given week. We had some rough times at first, but things settled in fairly quickly. Much to my surprise, they were not all that interested in earning a lot of the different things that I had offered, even though they had helped to pick out the options. However, what was a big surprise, the McDonalds lunch with me on each Friday became a pretty big deal. Every Thursday we voted as a class on who had earned it. And, you could not earn it on consecutive weeks. The voting was to be based upon someone who had an exceptional week and/or had done something new/better than they had ever done before. The students took this voting very seriously.

Some people might say that they were just motivated by the food, which is often true of teenage boys (the class was all boys). But, there were many other possible things that could have been earned that were food related. In time, it became clear that they wanted to earn this because they were motivated to outperform their peers. Also, much to my surprise, they were motivated to have lunch with me. I offered to let them take the lunch with them, but they always chose to eat with me and visit with me.

During these lunches, we talked about virtually everything from school to home to girls to cars and it was very clear that they were all motivated to succeed, but they were all afraid of success on some level or another. These boys had had very little success in their lives, and usually had family and friends who expected them to fail. We were able to talk about what it might take to achieve their goals. Many of these students had goals that involved a blue-collar type of job, from car mechanic to welder to plumber. These boys had no idea if they could ever achieve one of these jobs, and little belief that they could. We talked about the steps they would need to take in order to have a chance at any of these jobs, and we even researched the schooling needed.

One of these boys stuck out to me, given that he had been transferred into this program due to drug dealing at another school. He eventually told me that both of his parents had died and his elderly grandmother was raising him. His grandmother had very little money, so he was not able to dress like the other students and felt like an outcast. Therefore, he found an easy way to earn some money (we did talk about the fact that that is illegal).

During our conversations, I found out that he wanted to someday become a chef. After a bit of research, I found out that he would easily qualify for a scholarship to the local trade school. Then, we worked to prepare him to take his GED test (long story to why that made the most sense). He easily passed the test and went off to culinary arts school. He called a few years later to let me know he was the number two chef at a very good restaurant in town. He was motivated, clearly, but needed a bit of guidance.

So, when we see a student who is not performing, we need to remember that all children, all people, want to do well. Some just have a much more difficult path to doing well and being successful. Also, some children, some people, are missing guidance and examples to follow. Luckily, we have an opportunity to provide both of these for our students, if we stop thinking of problems as a lack of motivation and start seeing them as opportunities to intervene, to help, to teach.

**Reflection:**

Now that you have read the story and thought about the questions, it is time to reflect.

- What did you think about when you read this story?
- How can that help you in dealing with current and future students?
- How can that help you in dealing with current and future parents?
- How can that help you in dealing with current and future colleagues?
- What can you do differently starting today, to achieve better results (even if you started with good results)?

# Parent and Teacher Conferences

This is a story from the mother of a student with a disability, regarding her experience at parent/teacher conferences. It emphasizes the importance of providing positives and providing hope.

**Things to think about when reading this story:**

- As you read this story, can you relate to it personally?
- Have you ever worked with a student, colleague or parent who was similar?
- What messages did you send to that student, colleague, or parent verbally or non-verbally?
- How do you believe they remember you?
- How would you like to be remembered by them?
- What did you do to make their life better?
- What did you do that might not have made their life better?

## Parent and Teacher Conferences

Dear friends,

As we prepare to conference with parents about their kids, I wanted to share with you that my kid is "that kid." The one who can't sit still, keep his hands to himself or his mouth shut. The one rolling on the floor or drawing on the desk, probably in Sharpie. The one who gets sent to the hall, gets the pink slip(s) at recess. He's the one who pushes teacher's buttons to get a laugh from his classmates. So, he's also the one who makes teachers breathe deeply, maybe shake their heads, point to the hall, move his desk, write an infraction, keep him from the school picnic.

When my son started kindergarten, I got a call from his teacher telling me he was being a bully because he tried to make another student kiss a picture of a spider in a book. His first-grade teacher said to me "Every other child has been successful on this behavior contract, so…." (unspoken message was that my kid must be defective somehow). He was diagnosed with ADHD as a second grader and medicated as a third grader. In sixth grade his math teacher told me he was rude. His ninth-grade teacher got up during a meeting to wander around the room and lean against the wall to demonstrate how my son behaved in class. I joke that I have PTSD because anytime the school calls or I get an email with the subject line "check in" or just his initials, I want to cry. My mom heart breaks a little every time they describe him to me, for that is not the boy I love and am trying so hard to raise well.

My son is funny, spontaneous, curious, bright, and silly. He is always up for an adventure. He loves being outside, building things, and talking about cool shoes. He earned a black belt in Taekwondo last year. I share these things because I am sure that many of his teachers never knew those things.

Having experienced these tough times (and believe me, based on this weekend, we are not done with them yet) I look a little differently at my interaction with parents and how I talk with them. My words are powerful, as evidenced by the things that have seared themselves into my brain about my child. What would it have been like to hear that they liked him (and not have that followed by a "but")? What would it have been like to get an email that had only positives to say (helps to set the stage when you call me later for the inevitable mess-up)? What about a philosophy that he needs a break from seat work whether or not he "deserves" a break? Or maybe my child doesn't have to complete the whole worksheet (which would set his ADHD brain on overload and probably cause undesirable behavior) to demonstrate the skills learned? But above all, <u>what would it be like to know that my kid's teacher saw him beyond his behavior?</u>

When we share difficult things, or concerns with parents, we are much more successful when we can show them we do see their child beyond behaviors, that we see them as a whole child. A funny anecdote or something you share that you genuinely like about their child (with no buts) can set parents at ease. Even if it is as simple as noticing what they like to eat for lunch. They will be more likely to hear us if we start with empathy and compassion.

This is a quote from the book "Kids Deserve It" (by Todd Nesloney and Adam Welcome) that I read recently and I love it: "Our kids have far more issues to deal with at home than many of us realize. They want and need us to come to school every day, ready to surround them with love, encouragement, and hope."

I think parents need that encouragement and hope too!

Happy conferences everyone!

**Reflection:**

Now that you have read the story and thought about the questions, it is time to reflect.

- What did you think about when you read this story?
- How can that help you in dealing with current and future students?
- How can that help you in dealing with current and future parents?
- How can that help you in dealing with current and future colleagues?
- What can you do differently starting today, to achieve better results (even if you started with good results)?

# Believing in our Students as High Achievers

This story is about a school that changed their approach, believed in their students, helped their students to believe in themselves, and then achieved outstanding results.

**Things to think about when reading this story:**

- As you read this story, can you relate to it personally?
- Have you ever worked with a student, colleague or parent who was similar?
- What messages did you send to that student, colleague, or parent verbally or non-verbally?
- How do you believe they remember you?
- How would you like to be remembered by them?
- What did you do to make their life better?
- What did you do that might not have made their life better?

## Believing in Our Students as High Achievers

Often times we hear teachers say that college level advanced classes are only for the high achieving, top 3 % of students or what we call the "cream of the school." Students become high achieving because their parents expect them to achieve at higher levels and believe that they can meet high expectations. They do not let their kids sell themselves short.

What would happen if we educators all make this a non-negotiable, that we do not let any student sell themselves short and create opportunities for ALL students to access rigorous higher-level courses? Opportunity to learn is the single most determinant factor that effects student achievements.

When I started my career as an International Baccalaureate Diploma Programme Coordinator, I was shocked to see only 9 students pursued the IB Diploma (Students who take all 6 IB Classes). Of the 250 students who took one or more IB classes, only 130 students were of color (the school is 19% white). As a leader of Equity, one of my core values is to have courage to bring about change to ensure that ALL our students are served well. All students must have various avenues through which they can access college level courses and achieve. There must be equity in access.

Through an online survey given to staff and students, I identified factors that contributed to the opportunity gap. 72% of the students did not know about IB, 79% of the students reported there was no adult encouragement to take IB or AP, and there was no expectation at home of attending college. This broke my heart. Why are we doing this to our students? We're clearly not in this profession for the money. Are we too busy in our day to day lives to stop and think about our students who are not pushing themselves? Are we only educating students who want to learn and not instilling a love for learning in each and every student? A student on the survey said, "I have potential I just need more encouragement." Another said, "I have a very low self-esteem. When I don't understand many things, I prefer not to ask for help, but to struggle through it on my own…I do not trust others quite well. I take my time to know the person before I say things. All my life has been filled with sadness and bitterness. But my goals may be out of reach sometimes, people may say I will not be able to do it. I want to be many things, an engineer, a DJ, a music producer, etc. But some of these classes have little or nothing to do with that, personally."

The issues at hand were finding the right classes for the students. When we looked at our list of course offerings, we only had higher level classes, nothing that could interest our diverse learners. We adopted new courses that would appeal to our non-traditional students, serve our students from various backgrounds and our diverse learners such as IB Film, IB World Religions, IB Sports Exercise and Health Science, Information Technology in a Global society, IB Music, IB Art. The question then arose of how to inspire our students and have them believe in themselves that they can ALL succeed in a rigorous course.

We shared the survey results with the teachers, the teachers were appalled and made a promise to themselves- the need to move away from deficit talk and to using a more positive dialogue. We created policies such as admissions, Language, and assessment to provide clarity about the IB programme. I visited all classes (not just honors) to inform ALL students about the course offerings, course prerequisites, benefits of taking IB courses, and course expectations for each of the courses. Familiarity with courses made students comfortable with signing up for IB. I then sorted data on course requests for next year and came up with a list of students who did not sign up for an IB class. I had one on one conferences with students who were identified as having potential but did not sign up for IB.

Students who did not sign up due to lack of adult encouragement had very low self-esteem. I helped build students' confidence by identifying their strengths and motivating them to take the IB course that corresponds with their strength. One such example was of a student who received special education services. She did not read or write at grade level but was passionate about Art. Encouraging her to take IB Art class was a testament that even if the student is not at grade level, they can access a course that teaches them how think deeper & respond in an alternative medium. This helped build her self- esteem. She continued to take IB Art year 2 and went on to Arts College after graduation. This student's mom had tears in her eyes because nobody had ever talked to her child about being in an IB class. As she held my hand and said, 'Thank you for believing in my child" a chill ran through my spine. Why are we not doing this more often? Why are we letting our students sell themselves short? A kind word, an encouraging phrase, and an appreciative smile that acknowledges a student's hard work doesn't cost anything, but we get paid in millions when we hear a "Thank you for believing in me." Such is the power of language for language exerts hidden power, like a moon on the tides.

We increased access to rigorous courses across the board, not just the underrepresented & underserved students. With these efforts, we were able to close our opportunity gap by 103%. We created a belief system and structures that ensured the opportunity gap remains closed even today. Our students understand that they will fit into any IB class if they choose. Let's continue to advocate for equity of access and make a promise to ourselves – a promise that we ensure all our students believe in themselves by creating hope. When we close the hope gap, we close the opportunity gap; when we close the opportunity gap, we close the achievement gap.

**Reflection:**

Now that you have read the story and thought about the questions, it is time to reflect.

- What did you think about when you read this story?
- How can that help you in dealing with current and future students?
- How can that help you in dealing with current and future parents?
- How can that help you in dealing with current and future colleagues?
- What can you do differently starting today, to achieve better results (even if you started with good results)?

# Themes

As you read this book and the stories, and as you reflected, we asked you to think about themes. What are the things that tie these stories together? We are hoping that you found the following, and possibly more, during your adventure through our book.

1) Communication --- Effective communication can lead to much better results for everyone involved. Effective communication is seeing and hearing from the perspective of the other person and making sure to carefully monitor your own communication. Seeking to understand before seeking to be understood.

2) Results --- Your results, not beliefs, likes, or wants, will tell you if something has been effective.

3) Introspection --- We need to learn from our mistakes and the mistakes of others in order to grow and become better. In life, we are pretty much either growing in skills or declining in skills. So, make the choice to be actively seeking to grow in skills by being honest with yourself.

4) Thinking outside the box --- Not everyone needs the same stuff, and sometimes we have to be rather creative to meet the needs of those we are trying to help.

5) Trust and Relationship Building --- Building relationships and building trust can and will solve many problems, some before they can even start.

6) Intentions do matter --- What is in your heart will be seen by others. It doesn't give you a free pass to say or do stupid things, but instead makes the healing process easier and faster when we make mistakes (if what is in your heart is the good intention to help the other person).

# Appendix A: Belief Systems

Steve has worked with and trained staff from hundreds of school districts across several states, and has seen that belief systems are a major hurdle to overcome as we try to achieve better results for our children. The authors decided to add some modified content on belief systems from their other books on the topic as appendices.

We are all experiencing our own personal journey, and everyone's journey is unique. Learning how to determine whether or not a student needs more interventions, or if a special education referral is more appropriate, is a long learning journey. This journey is made easier or more difficult depending upon each person's willingness and ability to reflect on their acculturation, their beliefs, their actions (practices) and their results. This same type of journey is needed for our ability to work successfully with students of color, to increase proportionality in gifted/highly capable programs, and many other areas.

We are acculturated from the day we start to understand what is occurring around us, or earlier. Acculturation is combined with knowledge and this creates belief systems that eventually lead to actions and practices at work. Our practices lead to results, good, bad, or other. We know our results with regards to disproportionality are poor. We could use this to analyze many areas of life, though, like our (my) ability to maintain a healthy weight. Our results are not poor because we are actively and knowingly doing bad things (actions or practices), given educators are good and caring people. In order for us to achieve different results, we need to understand what is occurring with our belief systems and acculturation, and how these impact our practices. Then, we can modify our practices and achieve different results. Key questions each person needs to ask themselves, whatever the problem might be, are: "Am I part of creating or maintaining this problem? Or am I part of solving the problem? Our results on disproportionality (or fill in the blank) are very poor, what is my role? Can I possibly know the answer if I don't know the data for my school, district, and state?" Highly unlikely!

One principal that Steve worked with told him, "all of my best teachers are worried about not doing enough and not doing a good enough job and all of my weakest teachers believe they have nothing to learn and are working harder than everyone else." We (the authors) believe that when there is a situation at work (or in life) in which things do not go right or do not go well, the very first thoughts should be about the following: What could I have done differently? What could I have done better? What can I learn from this? This mindset is likely to lead to learning from our mistakes and remaining a learner throughout our career (and life for that matter).

Therefore, each of us needs to examine our belief systems and our acculturation, so we understand if we are helping to create some of the disproportionality or if we are part of maintaining existing disproportionality. This process is difficult and at times painful. However, it is necessary for us to figure out how we can be part of the solution, a goal each and every one of us should strive to achieve.

The following pages are meant to provoke thinking and to provide you with examples to help stimulate others' thinking. Hopefully this will also evoke emotions, as emotions help us to remember what we have learned. For example: a parent may try to teach their 3-4-year-old a new word that isn't important to the child, and the child just does not learn the new word. But when the parent gets cut off by another driver and responds, "$ *&^ @#$ $#@#," the child, only having heard this phrase once, uses it the following day in correct context, with correct intonation, and with emotion. Don't forget, this will happen in front of your parents, or friends.

So, as you read this, think about:

Acculturation (and knowledge learned) → Belief Systems → Practices → Results

Think about whether you are a part of creating, maintaining, or fixing the problems in your system, and what evidence you have to support your view of where you stand in your system. We are good and caring people, we can use our emotions to fuel a desire to learn more, change our practices, and support others to change their practices.

The reason for this is that our results occur not by chance, but as a result of our practices. Our practices occur based upon what we believe in and our belief systems are a combination of our knowledge and our acculturation. How we are acculturated creates a lens through which we see the world.

The stories on the following pages provide examples of this. We are sharing these with you to build knowledge and to encourage you to continuously monitor and challenge personal beliefs and practices.

**Overview**

1) **We See What We Are Acculturated to See:** Real world examples of acculturation creating a lens.
2) **Steve's Personal Educator Journey:** Real world example of developing over time, making mistakes, gaining new knowledge, learning, changing practices.
3) **Steve Hirsh's and Walter Gilliam's Research:** Research that shows the impact of our biases.
4) **Poverty:** Research that shows our results, and indicates biases.

## 1. We See What We Are Acculturated to See

The following three examples are meant to help you understand that we see what we are acculturated to see. Our acculturation provides a lens which we look through and that changes our view of the world.

Ushani is one of the few people on earth who is a German/Sri Lankan. Sri Lanka is an island in the Indian Ocean, just south of India. Therefore, it's easy to assume that Germans and Sri Lankans do not commonly meet one another in such a way that relationships are likely to begin. Additionally, of the Germans and Sri Lankans who do meet, not all of them speak a common language. Then, of the Germans and Sri Lankans who do meet and who do speak a common language, not very many are likely to form a romantic relationship, get married, and have children.

People who meet Ushani struggle greatly in figuring out her heritage and make many assumptions. Ushani has had numerous experiences in which someone has spoken Spanish to her, assuming that she is a Latina, only to have Steve respond. This tends to leave the person completely dumbfounded. They probably wonder why the Latina doesn't speak Spanish, but the older white guy does (some folks have literally told Steve that it is confusing to them to have an older white guy speaking Spanish with them). When Ushani is around people who are Black or African American, she is often thought to be a light skinned Black or African American woman. Then, there are times in which people believe that Ushani is a woman from India (to her Sri Lankan relatives, this is totally illogical). Virtually no one guesses that Ushani is from Sri Lanka. This is in large part because people rarely have a mental picture of what someone from Sri Lanka looks like (a lack of knowledge, a lack of this being part of one's acculturation). Did you have a picture of what someone from Sri Lanka might look like prior to this? Nobody ever guesses German, and many Germans struggle to "see"

Ushani as a German. Some Germans think she is Turkish; others think she is Black. Many years ago, when Ushani was still a young child, a friend of the family asked her mother, when she considered moving back to Germany, "Don't you think it will be difficult for a Black child to grow up in Germany?"

People are not acculturated to think of someone who looks like Ushani as German. Acculturation created lenses for each of these groups that impacted their decision making and their actions, like it does for all of us.

Steve usually uses the terms Latino(a) and Black, instead of Hispanic and African-American, given his acculturation. This is an important point about cultural competence versus cultural responsiveness. Someone asked Steve why he was doing this, questioning his cultural competence. This question led Steve to add discussion on this topic to all of his 1-day trainings.

In education, there has been a great effort to make people culturally competent, which is something Steve and others question. The concept of cultural competence is based on a belief that we can look at someone and tell by their appearance what culture they identify with and then apply our knowledge of that culture. Steve uses "Latino," given that his Spanish teacher uses the term Latino. However, he has talked to many people who could be Latina, Hispanic, Cubano, Peruana, Chicano, … about this very topic. Roughly 40% of the people Steve talked to identified as Hispanic and 40% Latino, with 20% not identifying as either, but instead as Cubano, Peruana, Chicano, … Also, Steve uses Black instead of African American, because two of his sons identify as Black, and not African American. Steve knows this because he asked them, independently, and they explained why they identify as Black and not African American. Steve also asked a co-worker the same question, and she identified as African American and explained why.

The point of this discussion is that we cannot know the cultural identity of someone by simply looking at them.

Furthermore, even if we could, there are at least 400+ cultures within our schools (we have over 400 languages in our schools and that translates into well over 400 cultures), and we could not possibly know specific details about every one of these groups (even if we could identify people by their appearance). Instead, we need to be culturally responsive. We need to pay close attention to the people we work with. We need to watch their body language, have the courage to tell people that we need their help in understanding their culture, and have the courage to tell people that we might make mistakes and that we want them to educate us.

The following example is from Steve's experience as a child with an extreme speech impediment and aphasia illustrates how acculturation and belief systems can create lenses through which people interpret the world. Steve's grandmother told him the following story many times. When Steve was 3 to 4 years old, Steve's parents were convinced by their friends that he must be "retarded," the term of the time. Eventually, his parents took him to Seattle Children's Hospital for an evaluation. The first person who saw Steve was a Speech and Language Pathologist, and this person told Steve's parents that not only was he not "retarded," he might actually be bright. That same afternoon Steve was evaluated by either Nancy or Hal Robinson (The Robinson Center on the University of Washington Campus) and Steve's parents were told he was gifted. A strange day in the life of a child who had no idea what was going on. The jury is still out regarding who was right (that is meant of be funny ☺).

During the time Steve's parents were convinced by others that he might be "retarded," even though, at an age of 3-4 years old, Steve was reading and playing chess with adults. Most folks were sure Steve was just looking at the books and they didn't believe his mother's claim that he was reading (given nobody could understand what he was saying). The chess was pretty hard to deny, since people could see it occur.

So, what is the point of this story? As a child Steve could not effectively communicate and was therefore seen by others to be cognitively limited, or "dumb." In our society, people who don't speak English are often seen as unlikely to be intelligent*. However, in our schools with language learners, it is possible that the smartest child in the school does not yet speak English.

*Steve has noticed during his training events that people in the audience who speak English as a second or later language all nod their heads in agreement when this point is made.

Have you ever seen an interview with Tiger Woods in which he talks about how much it bothers him that he is virtually never seen as an Asian man? Do you ever think of Tiger Woods as an Asian man? Or, solely as a Black or African American man? Tiger Woods expresses how he sees this as disrespectful to his mother and the heritage he has inherited from her.

There are many other examples in our world, yet this provides a window into how acculturation creates a lens through which we view our world. We need to examine ourselves to see how our acculturation is creating our lens.

## 2. Steve's Personal Educator Journey: The Painful Life Lessons

Throughout this book we asked you to reflect upon your thoughts, acculturation, knowledge, beliefs, practices and results. This is something that Steve has faced on several occasions during his career, and the following is an example of that. In life, we shouldn't ask others to do things we are unwilling to do ☺.

When Steve was in graduate school there was no coursework on the assessment of language learners; it was not even discussed. Steve began his career in the Tacoma School District and he quickly realized that he lacked skills in the area of evaluating language learners. Then he learned that finding information on this topic was next to impossible. This was pre-Google.

The first event to shape Steve's experience as a school psychologist in the area of language learners was a little boy who walked into his office with a doctor's script that said "ADHD, qualifies for special education as a student with an Other Health Impairment."

School psychologists often do not take this any better than medical doctors would take school psychologists making medical diagnosis and sending the families to the doctor's office. Steve called the doctor and asked him how he made the diagnosis, and the doctor responded, "I was educated at Harvard." After hearing this a few times Steve expressed his lack of care regarding the doctor's education. The doctor finally said, "I interviewed the family." Steve responded, "You speak Vietnamese?" The doctor then told Steve to do things that would be anatomically difficult to achieve, Steve responded, and eventually the doctor hung up the phone (it is likely Steve was having a better time than the doctor). It was later discovered that this student did not have ADHD and the family had no idea what had occurred.

Steve moved on with his career, eventually landing in a district that had a large percentage of Spanish speaking students in special education. Steve decided that he wanted to be bilingual and bi-literate, so he started taking night classes. After a year, he might have achieved the ability to ask where the bathroom is or order a beer, but not much more. With a great deal of luck, Steve ended up eating dinner with Dr. Stephen Krashen, one of the leading experts in the world on language acquisition. Dr. Krashen told Steve what he needed to do, and it was all about comprehensible input. So, Steve started to read books in Spanish, starting with kindergarten level books, until he mastered those, then first grade level books, and when he mastered those, second grade level books (reading The Mouse and the Motorcycle with great excitement), and so on.

Steve eventually had a dilemma. The only books at his level that he could find were the Twilight series, something rather hard on his ego (yes, this story is going somewhere). Steve thought he was safe reading this at school, and was walking to the staff lounge holding this book when a nice little girl that Steve knew well asked him if she could borrow the book after he was done with it. Steve first thought "Why?" believing she could not read the book because she was qualified for special education for reading, had never lived in a Spanish speaking country, and had no formal education in Spanish. Steve told her, "I will buy you brand new copies of the books if you stop by my office each week to, 1) Tell me about what you read, 2) Tell me about what you liked, 3) Tell me about what you think will happen next." This did not go as Steve thought it would go. Not only did she read every one of these books, she provided Steve replies to his questions ad nauseam. The point to this story is that not only was she qualified for special education for reading in English, not only had she never been formally educated in Spanish, not only was she reading at a higher level in Spanish than in English, Steve was the school psychologist who had qualified her for special education. This was a painful learning moment for Steve. A moment that required a lot of reflection.

Soon after this Steve began working for the Kent School District as the ESA Coach (the coach for all of the school psychologists, speech and language pathologists, occupational therapists, and physical therapists). He was offered the opportunity to start the district supported ELL graduate level program through Heritage University. This is where the work on the ELL Critical Data Process began, and the puzzle pieces started coming together.

The point of this is that each of us is on a journey of skills development. This can only occur if each of us is honest with ourselves about our mistakes, honest with ourselves regarding the impact of our acculturation, honest with ourselves about our skills (or lack of skills), honest with ourselves about our knowledge (or lack of knowledge) and if we do something to work on our own issues (Yoda said, "There is no try, there is do and not do"). We also need to be willing to examine our own issues around belief systems and race, in order to improve and focus on making a difference in disproportionality.

### 3. Steve Hirsch's Research

Steve Hirsch is a school psychologist in Washington State who has been a leader within the state school psychologist association for many years. Dr. Hirsch completed the following research as part of other ongoing projects and presented the information at the state school psychologist conference, trying to help people understand that we have biases that we are not aware of, and that those biases are impacting our work. The following slides represent the results after staff were given identical data on four students, in which the only difference was the name of the student and the country of origin.

The first of the following slides shows that, with identical data, the Latino students were significantly more likely to be referred for special education evaluations. The second slide, with identical data for each of the students, shows that there are significantly different rates of recommendation to complete an early re-evaluation for the possibility to exit the student from special education, based solely upon their race (due to the subtle and likely unknown biases of the participants). Given the data is identical, it would be hard to find another likely reason for the differences...

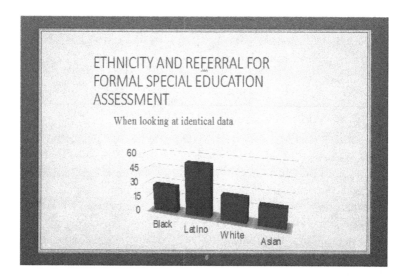

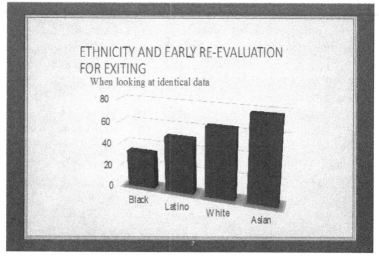

We all want to believe that we do not have biases, yet we all have them. It is a natural part of being human. However, we need to have the courage to examine our biases and the impact of those upon our work.

Another excellent example of research on biases is the research completed at Yale University by lead researcher Walter Gilliam. This research had a group of teachers watching videos of children playing, and they were asked to identify the challenging behaviors as they saw them occur in the videos. There were four children, one White boy, one White girl, one Black boy, and one Black girl. The researchers used eye scanning technology to watch the eyes of the teachers. The teachers watched the Black boys significantly more than the other children. The interesting part is that there was no challenging behavior at all occurring in the videos. The research has other very important components and is well worth reading (if you Google Walter Gilliam and research on biases you will find this and other research articles on this topic). As noted earlier in this book, Black boys are identified as behaviorally disabled at a much higher rate than other children. What if that is a result of school staff expecting them to behave poorly, watching them more closely than other children, and reacting differently given those expectations? Is it also possible that these children behave differently because they feel that they are being treated unfairly, singled out, and are constantly watched?

### 4. Poverty

When working with large groups of educators and asking the following question, rarely is there someone who is willing to raise their hand and say "yes":

Do people in poverty have higher rates of disabilities?

The answer is yes, but not based upon what some people might be thinking. The answer is yes because people with disabilities have higher rates of poverty. Reading deficits exist with roughly 80% of all students in special education. In our country, someone who cannot read, on average, is going to have a much more difficult time obtaining a living wage job. Therefore, there is some causation from disability to poverty, and a small correlation of poverty to higher rates of disability. Sadly, though, the research shows that students in poverty are frequently over identified for special education even though the correlations/causations noted above are about their parents and not about our students. And, poverty does not cause disabilities, but can be linked to less exposure and experience, and sometimes less time for parent support. These factors do not make a student disabled, instead create a situation in which a student is likely to have a more difficult time in school. The following pages document the research Steve completed in Washington State, showing that our qualification rates and our poverty rates are linked, sadly.

Steve examined the data from 295 school districts. No district was purposely left out of the data, with the exception of school districts in the data set that were(are) not actually comprehensive school districts (e.g., School for the Blind). Therefore, with a set of 250 districts, it is highly unlikely that any district missed would have impacted the noted trends.

For 16 districts the special education eligibility qualification percentages fell below 10% of the total student population. For 15 of these 16 school districts, the average student population in the districts was 145 students (145 is the average of the total student population and not just the total for the special education population; the 16th was a medium sized district noted separately below).

There were 32 districts with special education eligibility percentages above 18% of the total student population. The average student population across these districts was 392 students. As above, 392 represents the total student population and not just the special education population. The highest percentage of children qualified as children with disabilities was

37.5% of the district. Can there really be a district where 37.5% of the children have disabilities? That district happened to have a population in which 75% of the students were of Native American heritage. Did those two numbers happen together totally by chance? That is very unlikely and the results are inappropriate.

In the State of Washington, 45.9% of the students were on Free or Reduced Lunch at the time of this research. The average percentage of F/R Lunch for the districts below 10% special education qualification rate was 24%. The average percentage of F/R Lunch for the districts above 18% was 75.6%.

The only medium/large district with a percentage below 10% of the student population qualified for special education services was the Issaquah School District, at 8.8%. It is interesting to note that Issaquah School District has some of the highest state test scores noted during this research.

Although the F/R Lunch difference is extreme, there is no way to prove that it is a causal factor. Yet, many research studies have indicated that poverty is a very high predictor of special education qualification. This occurs even though it would be very hard to argue, beyond a minimal percentage difference, that poverty has any correlation to rates of disabilities, and no causal relationship either. It is important to note that the causal or correlational issues we are talking about refer to the parents of our children, not our children. Therefore, the correlation becomes even far weaker when looking at the children. That is, the small correlation of the parent in poverty to disability of the parent would be multiplied by the small correlation of parent to child disability (inheritance) to achieve a very small correlational value/predictive value.

It is interesting to note that virtually all of the districts on the extremes of the range have very small student populations. In all of these cases, one or only a few people are leading the qualification decisions.

It would be hard to examine this data and not see the human impact on the work. We have a lot of power in influencing outcomes, and, hopefully, a lot to think about in our daily work to bring about positive student outcomes.

You will see these points repeated throughout the book because we have a very hard time seeing ourselves involved in any of the negative results ("we" being that universal we). However, most staff have not examined the data for their schools and district. We need to have the courage to look closely at our work and to begin to solve problems as they appear. The data is not the way it is because so few people are involved in the problem. Wherever there is a problem, a lot of staff members were involved in creating or maintaining the problem (remember, not bad people, just bad results). This could seem to contradict what was said above. However, in the problem noted above just a few people had "control" over the outcome, yet many people had input and involvement. So, the big "we" could have stopped the problem if they had seen it as a problem. We need as many people as possible involved in the solutions.

The following quote from the University of Texas at Austin is included to provide additional insight into this issue.

Education and Transition to Adulthood, Information on Learning Disabilities, available at: http://www.utexas.edu/cola/etag/Related%20Sites/Learning-Disabilities.php

> *Although the research focus has primarily been on the disproportionate labeling of racial minorities with LD, the research team found that differences in the rates of being labeled are more dramatic by socioeconomic status (SES) than by race. The odds of being labeled with LD are much higher among low SES than high SES high school students, regardless of whether the student is Black or white. In fact, low SES white*

*high school students are as likely as low SES Black or Hispanic high school students to be labeled with LD, but much greater proportions of racial minorities are in that high-risk low SES group.*

*In contrast to Black and white high school students, high SES Hispanic high school students are as likely as low SES Hispanic high school students to be labeled with LD. <u>The team found that disproportionate labeling of Hispanic students with learning disabilities in high school is attributable to the over-labeling of language minorities.</u>*

*The team also found that students attending higher poverty schools are actually less likely to be labeled with LD, and that systematic differences in academic achievement by SES, race, and linguistic status are a major factor in disproportionality.*

Underline added for emphasis.

### "Takeaways"

1) **We See What We are Acculturated to See: Real world examples of acculturation creating a lens.** We each need to examine the impact of our acculturation on our belief systems, on our practices, on our results.

2) **Steve's Personal Educator Journey: Real world example of developing over time, gaining new knowledge, changing practices.** Self-examination can be painful, but we need to figure out what we don't know, combine that with our acculturation, and remain lifelong learners, painful as it will be at times.

3) **Steve Hirsh's and Walter Gilliam's Research: Research that shows the impact of our biases**. We all have biases, we need to examine how they are impacting our work, our results.

4) **Poverty: Research that show our results, and indicates biases.** This is more evidence that our biases, beliefs, and

acculturation impact our results. The more we know about where our problems are, the better we can focus on fixing our problems.

**Again, are you part of creating, maintaining, or solving the problem? Without strong knowledge of your data, how can you know?**

### Closing Thoughts on Belief Systems

During the editing of our third book, the question was asked, "How do you change what people believe?" As educators, we are caring individuals and lifelong learners. The problems, or poor results, within disproportionality are not occurring due to individuals purposefully doing harmful things to children. As we see the impact of our actions or inactions in this area we will be highly motivated to change the results. Working on belief systems and acculturation, although painful at times, will be something we do.

Knowing that belief systems are a combination of acculturation and knowledge, educators will look for the knowledge they need (some of which can be found in Steve's and Ushani's books) and other information contained in the books of the many individuals we refer to within our books. Then, you can use the processes within Steve's and Ushani's books to change practices, which lead to changes in results.

John Hattie is possibly the leading expert in the world on what is and is not effective within educational strategies (Hattie's books, like <u>Visible Learning</u>, are powerful and useful books to own). An effect size of .4 is basically what is expected, the .9 is a very large effect size, and the 1.57 and 1.62 are extremely large effect sizes.

The following are some examples found within his books or through Google searches:

-.34 for Mobility

-.02 for Summer Vacation

.19 for Co/Team Teaching

.47 for Small Group Learning

.53 for Scaffolding

.90 for Teacher Credibility

1.57 for Collective Teacher Belief

1.62 for Teacher Expectations of Student Performance

It is easy to see from this that beliefs have extremely powerful effects on our results. Also, having the knowledge, like that provided by Hattie, can sure save a lot of time, time that could be wasted on practices that are proven to have low impact on student learning.

Anthony Muhammad, author of several books, wrote the following in his book *Overcoming the Achievement Gap Trap*, "We cannot solve the problem until we look at it differently" (page 61) and "We cannot pursue equality when our value systems favor one group over another, especially when we lack the courage to even discuss the problem objectively" (page 75).

The work by Carol Dweck and her book on growth mindset versus fixed mindset is fantastic information for anyone in the process of evaluating and working on their own beliefs. It is also a great book for book study groups and the valuable discussions that can occur during book studies.

You have seen the problems, the issues about acculturation and belief systems, their impact on practice and results. It will take courage and knowledge to move forward. The good news is that better results lead to higher levels of satisfaction, so it will be worth it.

# Appendix B: A Different Lens

# LE³AP

**Look at:**

**Exposure**

**Experience**

**Expectations**

**and**

**Practice**

This appendix was added to allow the reader to see another way, or lens, in which to examine a presenting problem. Whatever the case, if you examine a student using this lens and then compare them to others who have the desired skill, you can determine if the problem/concern/lacking skill is reasonable given the Exposure, Experience, Expectation and Practice of the student who is struggling. This process can be added to any root analysis process that your team is already using.

The LE³AP process takes into account these four main areas, in order to understand whether the skill deficit in question is related to Exposure/Experience/Expectations/Practice or a possible disability. In other words, once a team has looked at a problem with the "lens" of exposure, experience, expectations and practice, does the presenting problem appear (all things considered) reasonable or does it appear to represent a potential disability?

These four areas are being differentiated as follows:

**Exposure:** The team looks at whether or not the student was exposed to the area of concern in a manner similar to students who have learned the skill/behavior in question.

**Experience:** Is differentiated by looking at whether or not the student was actively involved in the skill/behavior similar to students who developed the skill/behavior in question.

**Expectation(s):** Did the adults in the student's environment expect them to attempt/learn the new skill/behavior? How did they support that learning? And how do those expectations and support compare with what you would normally see for a child who has learned that skill/behavior?

**Practice:** Examines what the student (or adults) did in order for the child to get better at the skill/behavior and how that compares to students who have acquired the skill/behavior in question. Practice is a focused effort on improving a skill, not solely active participation in the skill/activity (e.g., working on phoneme skills development versus pleasure reading).

It is important to note that some students do not have exposure and/or experience given that they have a disability that limited their exposure and/or experience. For a student who clearly has a medical condition that impacts their access to their education or for a student who clearly has a cognitive impairment, a process like this should be abbreviated as appropriate (based upon the documented evidence). In this case, the process might become more about data gathering for the referral and potential evaluation process (based upon facts, not impressions).

The following five examples provide some context.

194

## Student 1:

This student was a 6<sup>th</sup> grade student who was performing well below grade level expectations. He is from a Russian background and he is one of nine siblings. The majority of his siblings were doing well in school, yet a few were doing poorly. All indicators were leading toward a special education referral. The school psychologist was in the process of interviewing the student's mother, and the information continued to support the possibility of a special education referral. Then, his mother stated, "You know he can read and write in Russian, right?" This information was not known to the team, so the school psychologist asked if they could use the interpreter to get an example of her son's reading and writing skills in Russian.

The student came into the school psychologist's office and the school psychologist opened a webpage in Russian, asking the student to read the information and provide a summary. The student did this and provided a detailed summary, and the interpreter stated that the summary was accurate. Then, the school psychologist wrote questions in English that the interpreter did not get to see. The student wrote responses to the questions in Russian and the interpreter read these. She stated that the written responses were easy to understand, just with some misspellings. The school psychologist asked the student's mother about the family's emphasis on English versus Russian. The student had attended 1 hour per week of class in Russian. The mother made it clear that it is very important to the family that the student learns to read and write in Russian, and that it is not so important that he reads and writes in English. They have a family business in which all of the boys are expected to work in, and they need to be able to speak, read, and write in Russian for the business.

**Exposure**: The student has been exposed to English since very early in his life.

**Experience**: The student has been in an English school since Kindergarten, and was participating at a low level.

**Expectations:** The family expects Russian skills to be learned and mastered, not English skills.

**Practice:** The student had a long history of completing very little work within the school setting.

Therefore, is it really reasonable to expect him to have grade level skills in English, knowing all of this???

And, a student who can read/write in their native language at a higher level than in English (with far less exposure and experience) is not a student with a learning disability.

**Student 2:**

A little boy or girl, 3 to 4 years of age, is having a very difficult time pronouncing their words, and does not appear to even be trying. When this child wants some cereal, their mom or dad or older sibling goes to the cupboard because the child is pointing that direction and grunting. Then, they open the cupboard and the adult (or older sibling) points to the first box. The child says, "untuh." The adult or older sibling points to the second box. The child says, "untuh." Then the third box, and the child responds, "unhuh." The adult or older sibling then pulls this box down, fills a bowl with cereal and gives it to the child. The child has had their needs met without using appropriate language skills.

**Exposure:** It is highly likely that the child has heard all of the correct words.

**Experience:** The child has not been using or attempting to use the correct words.

**Expectations:** The adults are not expecting the child to use or attempt to use the correct words.

**Practice:** The child is not practicing the needed skills, whether approximations that could be shaped or the actual words.

This child could be a child with a disability or non-disability developmental delay, yet it would be very difficult to accurately assess this skill set, not knowing what some intervention and work with the family could achieve.

### Student 3:

A fourth-grade boy was having a very difficult time with reading comprehension. His entire family (other than his siblings) spoke zero English and his family stayed within the Latino community to get all of their needs met. His parents are literate in Spanish, but had told him that they didn't want him learning to read in Spanish until after he had learned to read in English without problems. The team talked with the parents and the parents agreed to allow the school psychologist, who happens to read in Spanish, to work with him on Spanish reading skills. In about 6 weeks the boy was reading with comprehension, with most of the teaching focusing on letter sounds. He then was able to comprehend at a higher level in Spanish than in English. It turned out that his basic language skills (i.e., BICS) were primarily in Spanish and his academic language skills (i.e., CALP) were primarily in English. It was very difficult for him to use contextual clues while reading in English, given he was missing many of the words. Yet, in Spanish he knew the words and could use them to figure out the more difficult words using contextual clues.

**Exposure:** He was exposed to the English words.

**Experience:** He did not use them (academic words) much, given he had no use for them outside of school. Within the school setting, there are many words (daily words used in communication) that one is unlikely or less likely to use.

**Expectations:** Parents expected him to learn in English before developing the skill in Spanish.

**Practice:** There was no practice that was addressing the core problem, given that the core problem was not known.

This student benefitted greatly from the intervention that was focused on his actual need. This "practice" allowed him the opportunity to understand how to use contextual clues, using his stronger language. Then, he was able to transfer this skill into his work in English.

**Student 4:**

This student was also a fourth-grade student, and actually happened to be in the same classroom as student number 3. This student was having a very specific problem, he was struggling greatly with phonics and phonemes when reading. His parents were reading to him in Spanish and trying to work with him on these issues. His little sister (same environment as his) was in the second grade and already reading at a higher level than this student. Also, his parents were the only people in his world who spoke Spanish 100% of the time, his other relatives usually spoke English.

**Exposure:** He had been exposed to reading in English and had multiple years of intervention for the problems/concerns he was demonstrating.

**Experience:** He was trying to read in English and in Spanish, with support in both languages.

**Expectations:** His parents and school staff all had high expectations of him. His writing was at grade level if spelling was not taken into account, his math calculations was at grade level independently, and his math problem solving was at grade level when the problems were read to him.

**Practice:** He had had several years of intervention that was designed to target his problems with phonics and phonemes.

This student was referred for a special education evaluation. His problem was very specific in nature and was showing up across both languages. He had been exposed to the skill that he was not developing, he had experience with these skills, he was expected to learn these skills, and he was given an intervention (practice) designed to improve these skills. These facts, along with the fact that his sister (same environment, two years younger) was reading at a higher grade level than him, were all factors that helped determine that he was a student in need of special education services.

### Student 5:

Soon after arriving in the United States, a parent came into the school and made a special education referral for her son prior to his first day of school. The school psychologist visited with her and talked about how unusual that was, explaining that we normally allow the student to start school, that we try to get to know the student, and then determine an appropriate action plan. She explained, through an interpreter she had brought with her, that her son had autism and was severely impacted. She had a stack of medical records and reports (all translated into English), and she wanted a special education evaluation. The school psychologist asked her to bring him to school later that day, to get an opportunity to meet him. She was very hesitant, believing that this was a very bad idea. She did bring him into the school later that day, and the school psychologist observed that he was, indeed, extremely impacted due to his autism.

**Exposure:** This child had had very little exposure to school and to his new environment.

**Experience:** This child had had no experience with a school in the new environment.

**Expectations:** He was expected to behave appropriately and to attempt to learn, but at this time the impact of his autism limited his success greatly.

**Practice:** There was very little practice that was occurring, given it was very difficult to obtain and maintain his attention on the wanted behaviors.

This student did not have the exposure, experience, nor practice. However, he was severely impacted by his disability and the fact that he did not speak English was not the determining factor in this situation. He was qualified for special education services within 10 school days.

**Summary:**

These examples provide a glimpse into using the LE$^3$AP process. This framework is meant to help staff look at problems based upon examining what is reasonable or likely, given exposure/experience/expectations/practice. Also, these steps provide information that helps staff reason through the design of potential interventions, or develop reasoning for the referral process, and/or develop reasoning and data for the evaluation process. The final example demonstrates that, at times, the disability is the determining factor and not the lack of English language development. Our book *Special Education Referral or Not* focuses on the LE$^3$AP process for examining concerns in general and our book *The Ell Critical Data Process – Second Edition* uses this for examining issues with English learners.

# Appendix C: Biographies for Ushani and Steve

## Steve's Biography

Steve's first job in education, before he became a school psychologist, was as a driver's education teacher. Then, Steve had a wonderful opportunity to study school psychology and work at the university, so he followed that path.

Steve started his career as a school psychologist in a district with a large ELL population. There he realized how little he had learned about language learners prior to this experience. Over the years, he completed graduate work in ELL studies, eventually creating the ELL Critical Data Process. Most recently Steve was the ESA Coach (coaching school psychologists, speech and language pathologists, occupational therapists, and physical therapists on special education processes, laws and procedural issues) for the Kent School District.

As of writing this, Steve has trained over 8,000 educators on the process across more than 200 school districts in multiple states.

## Ushani's Biography

Ushani is a writer, artist and trainer who has worked for major corporations as a training manager. Ushani has been instrumental in the writing of our books, working diligently to ensure that the writing speaks to a wider audience.

Steve and Ushani (Steve's wife and co-author) have four books for sale on Amazon.com. The first book, *The ELL Critical Data Process – 2ⁿᵈ Edition*, is a resource for learning professionals for determining whether more interventions are needed or if a special education referral is a reasonable option. Their second book, *Evaluating ELL Students for the Possibility of Special Education Qualification* went into print in September of 2015, and focuses on the special education evaluation process for language learners and how to potentially achieve appropriate identification rates. Their third book, *Special Education Referral or Not*, is about using a matrix-based approach with non-language learners. Their fourth book, *ELL Teachers and Special Education*, is a self-study or group study course for ELL teachers to learn more about special education.

# Appendix D: Recommended Books

**Carol Dweck**

o   Mindset: The New Psychology of Success

**Steve Gill and Ushani Nanayakkara**

o   The Ell Critical Data Process – 2nd Edition:
    Distinguishing Between Disability and Language
    Acquisition

o   Evaluating ELL Students for the Possibility of
    Special Education

o   Special Education Referral or Not

o   ELL Teachers and Special Education

**John Hattie**

o   Visible Learning: A Synthesis of over 800 Meta-
    Analyses Related to Achievement

**Anthony Muhammed**

o   Overcoming the Achievement Gap Trap

**Benjamin Hoff**

o   Tao of Pooh

**Ross Green**

o   Lost At School (and other titles)

Cover photo: Goat Lake, Washington. To view the photo
correctly, turn the book 90 degrees to the left.